equipment and flycasting are included in the discussion. You'll also see the floats, sinkers, hooks, snap-swivels and other types of terminal tackle that are best suited for any fishing situation. Information on boats, depth finders, maps, navigation equipment and trolling equipment completes the section.

The final section, *"Basic Gamefish Techniques,"* is divided into 15 chapters, including largemouth bass, smallmouth bass, white bass and striper, crappie, catfish, walleye and sauger, northern pike and muskie, and stream trout. Each chapter begins by teaching you how to identify a species and then shows you where it exists with an up-to-date range map. You'll also learn where to look for the fish in a variety of water types. At the end of each chapter is expert advice on what specific fishing equipment is needed to pursue the fish and what artificial lure or natural bait choices normally produce the best catches. Expert tips for fishing each species are also included.

The section concludes with two pages dedicated to the proper landing, handling and releasing of fish. You'll learn why it's important to land fish quickly, how to hold them without removing their protective slime layer and how to properly revive them.

Some fishermen think the key to catching more fish is the hot new lure they saw advertised in a magazine ad or on a TV "info-mercial." Don't be fooled. The secret to improving your catch comes from increasing your fishing knowledge and then practicing what you've learned. Reading *Fishing North America* gives you the insight needed to be a more successful angler.

1

UNDERSTANDING
FISH
& THEIR ENVIRONMENT

Fish Senses

Fish are fine-tuned to their watery world. In addition to the usual senses of most animals – vision, hearing, taste and smell – they have a unique sense, the *lateral line*. It enables them to find food and detect danger even when they are unable to see.

LATERAL LINE. Nerve endings along a fish's sides (see crappie at right) sense vibrations in the water, helping fish determine the speed, direction of movement, and even size of predators and prey. In murky water, the lateral line is more important to a fish's survival than its eyes. Not only does it enable fish to find food and escape predators, it also helps them detect fixed objects and swim smoothly in compact schools.

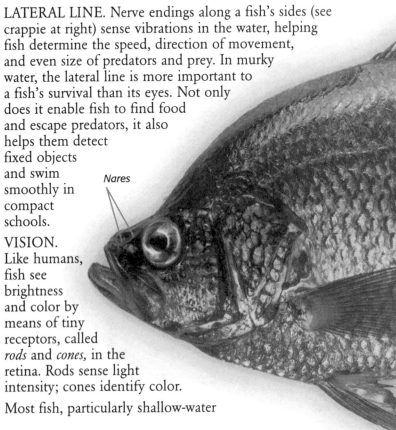

Nares

VISION. Like humans, fish see brightness and color by means of tiny receptors, called *rods* and *cones*, in the retina. Rods sense light intensity; cones identify color.

Most fish, particularly shallow-water

species like largemouth bass, have good color vision. In bright light near the surface, they can detect much the same range of color as humans. But some fish cannot see the full color spectrum. Walleyes, for instance, see all colors as some shade of red or green.

Water filters out color, so fish in the depths cannot see the spectrum of colors visible at the surface.

Red is first to disappear; yellow, next; and blue, last. Anglers working deep water soon learn that the most effective colors are usually blues and greens. Even if fish cannot see a certain color, however, they can still identify the object. They see it as a shade of gray, or they may respond to a flash of light reflected from it. This ability, combined with the lateral-line sense, explains why brightness and action of a lure are often more important than its color.

The distance fish can see in water depends on its clarity. In extremely clear water, fish can spot objects more than 100 feet away, but in very murky water, they can see only a few inches. The usual

Lateral line

range of vision for lake-dwelling fish is 10 to 20 feet.

Fish can see above-water objects through a *window* in the water's surface. Because of the way light rays bend when entering the water, fish can actually see above-water objects to the side of their direct line of vision. Therefore, anglers should keep a low profile when approaching fish, to keep from being detected.

Eye placement gives fish a wide field of vision. They can see in all directions, except straight down and straight back. To judge distance, a fish must turn to

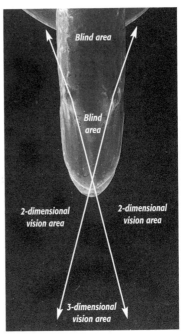

OVERHEAD VIEW of northern pike

view an object with both eyes. Some fish, like northern pike (above), have sighting grooves on their snout that broaden their field of three-dimensional vision.

Overhead objects are easy for most fish to see, even at night. A shallow-running lure shows up well against the surface; a deep runner is much harder to see at night because it does not stand out against the bottom.

HEARING. Fish hear sound with a system different from that used to detect vibrations. Although they lack external ears, they have an inner ear that functions much like that of a human. Tiny bones in the inner ear pick up sound, and semi-circular canals help maintain balance.

SMELL. Fish have a highly developed sense of smell. Odors are detected by the nasal sac inside the snout. Water is drawn into a front opening, or *nare* (see crappie p. 8), passed through the nasal sac and expelled through the back nare.

Salmon, hundreds of miles at sea, track the odor of water

from their home stream, enabling them to return to spawn at the precise spot where their lives began. Odors also alert fish to the presence of predators or prey. When attacked by a predator, baitfish emit a chemical that warns other baitfish to flee. In a laboratory experiment, a small volume of water from a tank containing northern pike was poured into a tank containing perch. The perch immediately showed signs of distress and scattered. Spawning salmon will retreat downstream when they detect the water-borne odor of a human or bear.

Despite their ability to detect odors, most predator fish rely more heavily on other senses to find food. Odors dissipate slowly in water, and if the current is from the wrong direction, the odor won't be detected at all. Vision and the lateral-line sense, on the other hand, enable fish to detect prey almost instantaneously.

TASTE. The sense of taste is of minimal importance to most gamefish. Notable exceptions are bullheads and catfish. Their skin, and especially their whiskers, or *barbels*, have taste-sensitive cells that enable them to test food before eating it.

Scent products are controversial among fishermen. Some believe they're effective on all fish species; others say only scent-oriented fish, like catfish, respond to them.

HOW SENSES AFFECT FISHING STRATEGY

Understanding the senses of gamefish and adjusting your fishing tactics accordingly will definitely improve your success. For instance, experienced anglers avoid banging their tackle box on the boat floor because they know fish can easily detect the sound and vibration. Bass anglers use lures with rattles to attract largemouths in muddy water, and pike anglers rely on flashy baits in clear water. Trout fishermen, understanding the concept of the fish's window, stay low when approaching the streambank. Channel catfish anglers, knowing their quarry has a strong sense of smell and taste, use stinkbaits – the smellier the better.

Food & Cover

Fish learn by trial and error what is edible and what is not. Young fish approach unfamiliar food with caution and often eject the morsel several times before swallowing it. But once they learn what is acceptable, they become much less cautious about eating similar items.

Over their lifetime, fish build up a long list of acceptable foods and, among these, a set of preferred items. However, many of their favorite foods, such as insects, are usually available for only brief periods. At other times, fish cannot afford to be so choosy and must eat whatever nature will give them.

HOW FOOD AFFECTS FISH BEHAVIOR

Baitfish hatched in spring become large enough to interest predator fish by midsummer. This explains why fishing slows down in the latter part of the summer and remains slow well into the fall. Then, fishing begins to pick up again as predators reduce numbers of young-of-the-year baitfish.

Insect hatches may cause fish to temporarily change diets. Walleyes, for example, may stop eating perch and switch to mayfly nymphs.

Windblown algae can be a clue to fish location. Baitfish grazing on algae attract larger fish that do not hesitate to feed in the shallow, discolored water.

UNDERSTANDING THE FOOD CHAIN

Algae, or *phytoplankton,* are tiny plants that constitute the basic link in the aquatic food chain. They come in many shapes. Zooplankton are tiny animals that graze on algae.

Minnows and other small fish eat zooplankton. Some fish,

however, bypass this link in the food chain by feeding directly on algae.

Small predators, such as crappies, consume minnows and other small fish. However, they may feed directly on large zooplankton.

Large predators, like northern pike, eat whatever food is available. Most prefer slim-bodied prey, because it's easy to swallow. But when such food is scarce, they do not hesitate to take deep-bodied prey.

HOW FISH USE COVER

From the day fish hatch as fry, they are constantly tested on their ability to survive. They need cover to avoid larger fish, fish-eating birds, aquatic mammals and other predators. Even with good cover, nature takes a heavy toll. Some fish lay as many as 100,000 eggs. Less than one-third may hatch and, of these, only 3 or 4 fish may reach adulthood. Adult fish use cover to help protect their nests, so that they do not have to guard all sides of it.

Adult fish also require cover to escape predators. Perch, for example, hide in weeds to avoid walleyes and northern pike. Weeds also help camouflage perch, so they can dart out to grab minnows or other prey.

Many kinds of fish move from shallow to deep water on a daily basis. This explains why cover adjacent to deep water generally holds more fish than cover far up on a shallow flat.

Another basic rule: broad-leaved weeds make better cover than narrow-leaved varieties. They provide more shade and better concealment from predators. Narrow-leaved weeds usually hold only small fish. Similarly, newly flooded trees, with all the small branches intact, make better cover than older trees, with most of the small branches rotted away.

Cover is just as important in moving water as it is in still water. Boulders, logs, bridge pilings or any objects that break the current and create eddies are gamefish magnets.

Where it is legal, fishermen often sink coniferous trees or brush piles to attract fish. Another option is to build an artificial fish attractor, such as a stakebed, which is built with 1x2 uprights attached to a 4x8-foot frame made from 2x4s.

Freshwater Basics

Fresh waters differ in many ways. Color and clarity are two conditions which can be easily seen. Less obvious, though more important to fish, are temperature, oxygen level and fertility. Together, these factors determine the type and amount of fish in a lake and what part of the lake they inhabit.

TEMPERATURE. Each fish species requires a certain range of water temperatures in which to live, grow and reproduce. Fish fall into three categories, according to temperature preferences (see chart opposite page). *Coldwater* fish are limited to lakes that provide a refuge of cold, oxygenated water in the heat of summer. *Coolwater* species fare best in waters with intermediate summer temperatures, but without long periods of high temperatures. *Warmwater* species thrive in lakes where temperatures are high all summer.

OXYGEN. The water in which fish live must have ample dissolved oxygen. Water absorbs oxygen when it comes in contact with the air. This is why flowing waters rarely have low oxygen levels. Oxygen is also added by aquatic plants. Fish extract oxygen as water passes through their gills. Crappies, northern pike, perch and especially bullheads tolerate lower oxygen levels than most gamefish.

FERTILITY. The fertility of any body of water is determined mainly by the amount of dissolved nitrogen and phosphorus. Just as the amount of fertilizer in the soil determines crop yields, the fertility level of a body of water determines how many pounds of fish it can produce. Fertile lakes have high levels of these nutrients; sterile lakes, low levels. The higher the fertility level, the heavier the algal bloom. Because algae is the basic link in the aquatic food chain, fertile lakes produce the largest fish crops.

Fertility also determines the kind of fish a body of water can support. Coldwater fish like trout cannot survive for long in fertile lakes. Dead plants and algae are rapidly decomposed by bacteria, which consume large amounts of oxygen, forcing the fish into shallow water. There, the high temperature would soon kill coldwater fish.

14

In shallow, highly fertile lakes, oxygen is used up rapidly in winter, and in years of heavy snow cover, aquatic plants do not receive enough sunlight to replenish the supply. Eventually, the lake undergoes *winterkill,* commonly called "freeze-out," and nearly all the fish die from oxygen starvation. High-fertility lakes are common in nutrient-rich farmlands, where fertilizers are routinely applied. Runoff carries the nutrients into nearby lakes, where they fuel heavy algal blooms. Low-fertility waters are usually surrounded by bedrock or nutrient-poor lands. Rains carry in few nutrients to fuel algal growth, so the water stays clear and fish production is low.

FERTILITY LEVELS of lake types are reflected by the amount of algae, which, in turn, determines the kinds of fish life. For examples, lake trout and cisco prefer sterile conditions; northern pike, walleye and smallmouth bass prefer moderately fertile conditions; largemouth bass, carp and bullhead prefer fertile conditions.

GAMEFISH TEMPERATURE PREFERENCES (Degrees F)

GAMEFISH SPECIES	TEMP. PREFS.	GAMEFISH SPECIES	TEMP. PREFS.
Lake Trout	50	Northern Pike	70
Brook Trout	54	Smallmouth Bass	70
Chinook Salmon	55	Crappie	71
Coho Salmon	55	Striped Bass	72
Cutthroat Trout	55	Largemouth Bass	73
Rainbow Trout	55	Bluegill	75
Brown Trout	60	White Bass	76
Muskellunge	67	Bullhead	78
Yellow Perch	68	Channel Catfish	78
Walleye	69	Flathead Catfish	80

▨ Coldwater   ▨ Coolwater   ▧ Warmwater

Temperature preferences of common gamefish species are shown above. But fish are not always found in water of the preferred temperature. If food is more plentiful in warmer or cooler water, that's where the fish will be.

Seasonal Movements

As the seasons pass, fish adjust to natural changes in lakes, reservoirs and ponds. Fish movement is keyed to two factors: dissolved oxygen and water temperature. Throughout the year, fish seek the zone in a lake that comes closest to satisfying both of these needs.

To understand how lakes change, it is important to know what happens to water at different temperatures. Water, like most substances, becomes lighter when warmed and heavier when cooled. But water has a unique property. When it cools below 39°F, it becomes lighter. This ensures that a lake's bottom water stays warmer than the surface during winter.

Because of this property of water, most lakes form three separate layers in summer. The upper layer, called the *epilimnion*, is warmer, lighter water that is easily circulated by the wind. As it mixes, it renews its oxygen supply. Meanwhile, the cold, heavy bottom layer, or *hypolimnion*, becomes stagnant and may lose its oxygen. Separating the two layers is the *thermocline*, a zone where the temperature drops very fast. In very shallow lakes, however, these layers may not form because the entire body of water is mixed by the wind.

The copy on the following page explains the annual cycle of a moderately fertile lake in a northern climate. Seasonal fish movement is different in other types of lakes. For example, infertile lakes do not lose oxygen in the depths, so fish are not forced into the shallows in summer or winter.

In extremely fertile lakes, low oxygen levels restrict fish to the shallows most of the year, with the exception of spring and fall turnover periods, when they may be found anywhere.

EARLY SPRING. The ice has melted. Runoff and the sun's rays rapidly warm a thin layer of water at the surface. As it warms, it absorbs oxygen from the air. Fish are drawn to the warm, oxygen-rich shallows.

Annual Cycle of a Moderately Fertile Lake

EARLY FALL. Cool nights lower the surface temperature. The margin between epilimnion and thermocline is less distinct. The hypolimnion remains unmixed and without oxygen. Many fish move to the cool shallows.

SPRING TURNOVER. When the surface water warms to 39°F, it sinks. Soon all water in the lake is 39°F, so density is the same from top to bottom. Wind easily mixes the water, spreading oxygen. Fish may be anywhere.

FALL TURNOVER. The surface water cools even more and begins to sink. The thermocline disappears. Soon, water at the surface is the same temperature as bottom water. Wind mixes the layers, scattering fish.

LATE SPRING. Warmer, lighter surface water starts to separate from cooler, heavier water below. Bottom water has oxygen, but is too cold for most fish. A strong wind can still mix the lake and scatter fish to any depth.

LATE FALL. The entire lake continues to cool, though faster at the surface. As the surface water drops below 39°F, it becomes lighter, so it floats on the warmer, deeper water. Fish move to the warmer water.

EARLY SUMMER. Three distinct layers form: the epilimnion, or warm surface layer; the hypolimnion, or cold bottom layer; and between them, the thermocline, where temperature drops fast. Fish select a comfortable depth.

EARLY WINTER. Ice forms on a cold, still night, though the lake may reopen if milder days return. Fish may be found at any depth, but most stay in deep water where the temperature is warmer.

MIDSUMMER. Temperature layers become more distinct. The deepest part of the hypolimnion begins to lose oxygen. Coldwater fish are forced into the upper part of the hypolimnion, even though the water is too warm.

MIDWINTER. Thick ice and snow reduce the amount of sunlight reaching aquatic plants, so they cease to produce oxygen. Decaying plants and animals on the bottom consume oxygen, forcing fish to the oxygen-rich shallows.

LATE SUMMER. Surface water has enough oxygen, but is too warm for many fish. The hypolimnion has lost much of its oxygen. Coldwater fish edge into the thermocline where warmer temperatures may kill them.

LATE WINTER. Ice and snow cover grows thicker. The low oxygen band widens. Soon, only the extreme upper layer has enough oxygen. A late winter thaw may bring oxygen into the lake. If not, it winter-kills.

Types of Water You Fish

Natural Lakes

Every natural lake is unique, the end product of a host of factors that combine to shape its character, including its fish population. Important elements are geographic location, size and shape of the basin and water fertility, which is the basis for the lake-classification system that follows.

OLIGOTROPHIC LAKES. Because the lands surrounding oligotrophic, or infertile, lakes release few nutrients, the water is quite sterile. Most oligotrophic lakes are located on the Canadian Shield, a vast rock-bound area that covers eastern Canada and dips into the northern states from Minnesota to Maine. Some oligotrophic lakes are found at high elevations, where the climate is cold. Coldwater species, such as trout, predominate. Because their fish are slow to grow and mature, these lakes can withstand only light fishing pressure.

MESOTROPHIC LAKES. These lakes of intermediate fertility are located primarily in the northern United States and southern Canada. However, they can be found most anywhere on the continent. Coolwater species predominate, though most support warmwater species, as well. A few have populations of coldwater fish.

EUTROPHIC LAKES. These fertile lakes are surrounded by nutrient-rich soils that add large amounts of nitrogen, phosphorus and other fertilizing elements. They are typically found in agricultural areas in the southern two-thirds of the United States, although there are many in the North.

Eutrophic lakes are best suited for warmwater species, such as bass and sunfish.

Every lake is oligotrophic when first formed. But as time passes, aquatic plants and animals die and their remains form a layer of organic ooze on the bottom. As this layer thickens, the lake becomes shallower and is more easily warmed by the sun. Plant growth increases, and the water becomes more fertile, edging into the mesotrophic category. As ooze continues to accumulate, the lake becomes eutrophic. Eventually, the water becomes too shallow for fish. This process, called *aging*, may take thousands of years.

Below are some of the most common types of natural lakes, ranging from infertile to very fertile.

COMMON TYPES OF NATURAL LAKES

TROUT LAKES are deep and cold, with very low fertility. They usually have rocky basins with sparse weed growth. Some are stocked with stream trout; others, including many in the Far North, have natural lake trout.

TWO-STORY LAKES are slightly more fertile than trout lakes, with basins of rock, gravel and sand, and sparse to moderate weed growth. They have trout in the depths and coolwater or warmwater fish, such as walleyes or small-mouth, in shallower water.

WALLEYE LAKES are moderately fertile, and their basins are sandy, with patches of gravel or rock. Weed growth is moderate. They support a diversity of warmwater and coolwater species, including walleyes, northern pike, bass and panfish.

BASS-PANFISH LAKES are somewhat more fertile than walleye lakes, with a higher percentage of mud bottom and heavy weed growth. Largemouth bass, sunfish and northern pike predominate. If walleyes are present, they're usually stocked.

ROUGHFISH LAKES are highly fertile, with mud bottoms and only small patches of sand or gravel. Algal blooms reduce water clarity to the point where plants grow only in the shallows. Bullheads and carp are dominant, but there may be some bass and panfish.

Ponds & Pits

About one-fourth of all freshwater fishing is done in these small lakes, most of which are man-made. There are nearly 3 million farm ponds in the United States alone, constructed mainly for cattle watering, irrigation or erosion control. Most ponds are made by bulldozing or blasting a basin, or by damming a small stream. Ponds are also created by beavers damming small watercourses, and by floods digging scour holes adjacent to streams.

Pits are generally deeper than ponds. They fill with water after various types of sand-gravel or mining operations have been discontinued. Strip-mining for coal, for instance, often leaves pits more than 50 feet deep. Iron-ore pits may be more than 500 feet deep. Most shallow ponds and pits are stocked with warmwater species, particularly largemouth bass, catfish and panfish. Deep ponds and pits can support trout if there is sufficient oxygen in the depths. Shallow ponds and pits can be managed for trout only if they are spring-fed. Even then, they may have to be aerated in winter.

COMMON TYPES OF PONDS & PITS

FARM PONDS are commonly stocked with largemouth bass and bluegills. Channel catfish are popular in southern farm ponds. As a rule, any pond that freezes over in the winter should be at least 12 feet deep over one-fourth of its area to prevent winterkill. Shallower ponds can be aerated to prevent wintertime fish kills.

BEAVER PONDS along coldwater streams often hold trout; those along warmwater streams, a mixture of species, such as bass, pike, sunfish and crappies.

GRAVEL PITS and quarries usually have clear, relatively infertile water. Deep pits are sometimes stocked with trout; shallower ones, bass and bluegills, or catfish.

STRIP PITS may be stocked with bass and panfish, trout or even catfish. But many newer pits are fairly unproductive, due to their steep banks and acidic water.

IRON-ORE PITS often have an ample supply of deep, cold, well-oxygenated water ideal for growing trout and even salmon. Shallower pits usually hold bass and panfish.

Man-made Lakes

Also called *reservoirs* or *impoundments,* man-made lakes are formed by damming rivers. In some respects, man-made lakes are much like natural lakes, but in other ways, they're very different. Like natural lakes, they often stratify into temperature layers. And they can be classified by fertility (p. 14) in the same way as natural lakes. But unlike natural lakes, reservoirs seldom lack oxygen in the depths, because of the moving water.

Man-made lakes tend to be longer and narrower than natural lakes, and there is usually a noticeable current at the upper end. The current carries in large quantities of sediment, meaning that their basins fill in much more quickly than those of natural lakes. Fluctuations in river flow cause dramatic changes in water level, meaning that aquatic plants are less abundant and baitfish crops less stable than in natural lakes.

The most common types of man-made lakes throughout North America are described below.

COMMON TYPES OF MAN-MADE LAKES

EASTERN MOUNTAIN RESERVOIRS are found in hilly or mountainous terrain. These deep, steep-sided lakes may be called hill-land, highland or cove reservoirs. The main lake is more than 100 feet deep and the creek arms may be several miles long. These waters are best suited to warmwater fish like largemouth and smallmouth bass, crappies and stripers, but some deeper ones also hold trout.

FLATLAND RESERVOIRS are surrounded by flat or gently rolling land and typically have depths of only 30 to 60 feet over most of their area. The main basin is relatively wide, and the creek arms short. These fertile lakes usually have good populations of largemouth bass, crappies, sunfish, catfish and white bass.

SWAMPLAND RESERVOIRS have maximum depths seldom exceeding 25 feet. These warm, weedy, highly fertile lakes are often low in clarity. They support the same fish species as flatland reservoirs, but the fish run shallower because of the low clarity and lack of oxygen in the depths. These lakes seldom have distinct creek arms.

CANYON RESERVOIRS have a long, narrow main body more than 200 feet deep, and long, narrow creek arms. These lakes, which are cold, clear and low in fertility, have sharp-sloping shorelines and are better suited to rainbow, brown or lake trout than to warmwater fish like largemouth bass. Between spring and fall, canyon reservoirs may be drawn down more than 100 feet to generate power.

PRAIRIE RESERVOIRS have warm, shallow, fertile water on the upper end and deep, cold, infertile water on the lower, so they support a wide variety of fish life, ranging from catfish to salmon. Creek arms tend to be small and short. Water levels fluctuate greatly, depending on long-term rainfall cycles.

DESERT RESERVOIRS, found in the Southwest, are at least 100 feet deep. They have a large storage capacity for supplying water to cities and agricultural areas. Rich desert soils make the water quite fertile. Most desert reservoirs have good numbers of largemouth bass, with some white bass, crappies, catfish, smallmouth bass or striped bass.

CANADIAN SHIELD RESERVOIRS usually have bedrock basins and are very low in nutrients. Most are deep and cold, with a highly irregular bottom and numerous islands and reefs. Many such reservoirs have "two-story" fisheries, with warmwater fish like walleyes and northern pike in the upper layer, and coldwater fish like lake trout in the lower.

Rivers & Streams

Beyond every bend in a river or stream lies a new fishing challenge. One moment, the water may flow slowly over nearly level ground; the next, it may turn into a churning *rapids* as it plummets over steep terrain.

Most streams and small rivers have these three distinct habitat types.

RIFFLES. Moderate to fast current and a turbulent surface are typical features of riffles. They have bottoms of gravel, rocks or boulders and are less than 2 feet deep. Extremely fast, whitewater riffles are called rapids.

RUNS. Runs are similar to riffles, but are deeper and less turbulent.

POOLS. Slow current and a surface that appears smooth on a calm day identify pools. They have bottoms of silt, sand or small gravel. Shallow pools are often called *flats*.

The riffle-run-pool sequence may not be as noticeable in very large streams or streams with a very slow current. Nevertheless, fish recognize the different habitat types and so can the angler with a well-trained eye.

RIFFLES, RUNS AND POOLS are formed by the awesome excavating force of moving water. Fast water in a riffle digs a deeper channel or run. As the run deepens, the current slows, forming a pool. The slower current causes sediment to settle at the pool's tail or downstream end. As sediment builds up, the water becomes shallower, channeling streamflow into a smaller area. Once again, the current speeds up, forming a new riffle. In most streams, this pattern is repeated about once for every seven stream widths. In other words, a new riffle, run and pool sequence would be repeated about every 140 feet in a stream 20 feet wide.

Species such as largemouth bass, crappies, catfish and walleyes spend most of their time in deep pools. Smallmouth bass and trout also inhabit pools but may be found in runs if the current is not too swift. Riffles are usually too shallow to provide enough cover for large fish, although they are important morning and evening feeding areas for many river species. Small gamefish and minnows stay in riffles through the day.

The slope or *gradient* of the streambed is one of the many factors that determine what kind of fish live in a particular river or stream. Others include water quality, bottom type and depth. The overriding factor, however, is water temperature.

Warmwater streams are home to such species as largemouth and smallmouth bass, white bass, walleyes, catfish and carp. Coldwater streams are best suited to species like trout, steelhead, salmon, grayling and whitefish.

Coldwater streams are often broken into two categories depending on fertility level of the water. *Limestone* streams

MAINSTEM RIVERS, found mainly in the Midwest, have been dammed to create a series of stair-step pools. Bordering the main channel is a complex network of backwater lakes, sloughs and connecting channels. Because of this habitat diversity, these large rivers support a wide variety of warmwater gamefish and roughfish species.

are normally fed by underground springs rich in calcium carbonate. Because they have an abundance of aquatic vegetation, insects and crustaceans, limestone streams grow more and bigger fish than *freestone* streams, which have a low mineral content.

Depending on which expert you listen to, there may be as many as 50 distinct types of rivers and streams in North America. But the types discussed below are most important to anglers.

COMMON TYPES OF WARMWATER STREAMS

SOUTHERN LARGEMOUTH RIVERS have warm, slow-moving, discolored water and a silty bottom. They may support crappies, sunfish, catfish and stripers, in addition to largemouth. Bordering the main channel are sloughs at the mouths of tributary streams, and oxbow lakes that remain after the river has changed course.

NORTHERN SMALLMOUTH STREAMS have clear, unpolluted water, moderate current and a fish population that usually includes walleyes and northern pike, in addition to smallmouth bass. There are few, if any, backwater areas, so the fish are usually found in deep pools and around cover within the main channel.

CANADIAN PIKE RIVERS usually flow through spruce bogs and tamarack swamps that give the water a bog-stained appearance. The cool water, moderate current and rocky bottoms are ideal for pike and walleye, but may also support brook trout, whitefish and even lake sturgeon.

GREAT LAKES TRIBUTARIES draw huge spawning runs of fish, such as salmon, steelhead and walleye, that inhabit the big lakes. Some streams also have resident populations of walleye, northern pike, muskie and smallmouth bass.

These waters vary greatly in character, ranging from small, clear streams to big, muddy rivers.

WESTERN CORRIDOR RIVERS serve as a pathway for salmon, steelhead and other migratory fish on their way to spawning grounds. Some such rivers have resident populations of smallmouth bass, walleyes and catfish. The clear, rocky, fast-moving water is not cold enough to support trout and salmon year-round.

TIDEWATER RIVERS, located in coastal areas, fluctuate greatly because of ocean tides. The downstream reaches are salty, the middle reaches, brackish and the upstream reaches, fresh. Most support freshwater fish, like largemouth bass and sunfish, and have seasonal runs of saltwater fish, such as striped bass and American shad.

COMMON TYPES OF COLDWATER STREAMS

FREESTONE streams are fed mainly by surface runoff and snowmelt. Low-gradient freestone streams flow slowly over sandy and silty bottoms. High-gradient streams flow quickly over long sections of boulders and broken rock. Freestone streams carry few nutrients and are not very fertile unless they have several feeder streams bringing in nutrients.

LIMESTONE streams are spring-fed. Low-gradient limestone streams flow slowly over sand, silt or gravel streambeds. Medium-gradient streams flow quickly over gravel, rubble or boulder streambeds. Many limestone streams flow over exposed bedrock and are often very fertile, with large populations of insects and crustaceans.

SPRING CREEKS arise from groundwater sources. They have slow to moderate current and very clear water. The stable water level allows development of lush weed growth and heavy insect populations. Some spring creeks teem with crustaceans and grow surprisingly large trout.

TAILWATER STREAMS, fed by cold water from the depths of a reservoir, often hold large trout populations. The best streams have stable flows, allowing development of rooted plants that hold many aquatic insects. Streams that fluctuate due to power generation are less productive.

2

FISHING EQUIPMENT

& HOW TO USE IT

Rods & Reels

Fishing rods and reels can be divided into the five basic categories shown below, and within each of those groups are many subcategories, based on specific kinds of use. Bass fishermen, for example, often carry a selection of different baitcasting outfits for such uses as pitchin', flippin', crankbaiting and grub fishing. Similarly,

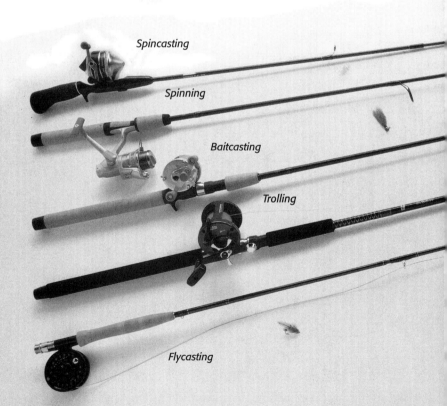

Spincasting

Spinning

Baitcasting

Trolling

Flycasting

many walleye fishermen carry different spinning outfits rigged for slip-sinker fishing, slip-bobber fishing and jigging.

Your rod and reel selection depends not only on the size of fish you'll be catching, but on the size of your lure or bait. A tiny, lightweight spinner, for instance, would be easy to cast with a light spinning outfit and 4-pound monofilament line, but casting would be nearly impossible with a heavy baitcaster and 17-pound monofilament.

As anglers gain experience and their fishing interests diversify, their inventory of rod-and-reel combinations usually grows. It's not unusual for avid anglers to own more than a dozen fishing outfits.

The basic information that follows is intended to help you select the type of fishing outfit that best suits your needs:

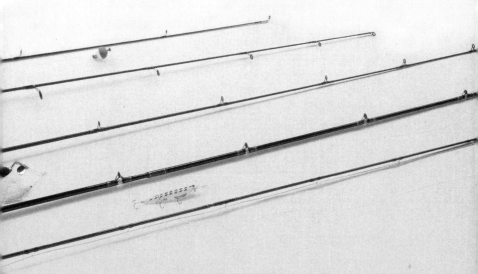

SPINCASTING. Many inexperienced anglers prefer spincasting gear, because it's backlash-free and the enclosed spool prevents much of the snarling associated with spinning gear. But the closed face also increases line friction, reducing casting distance. Spincast reels also have low gear ratios and, as a result, they don't retrieve a lot of line with each turn of the handle, which makes it very difficult to properly fish lures such as spinnerbaits and buzzbaits. While spincasting outfits are excellent tools to teach beginning anglers the mechanics of casting, fishermen should begin learning how to master spinning and baitcasting equipment as soon as possible.

SPINNING. Ideal for distance casting and tossing light lures, a spinning outfit includes an open-face reel, which has a *bail* that flips open to allow line to flow easily off a fixed spool. The rod has large guides to minimize line friction. Spinning tackle is highly versatile, and with no rotating spool, it cannot backlash. It is not the best choice, however, when using heavy monofilament line, which tends to spring off the spool and cause tangles.

BAITCASTING. Baitcasting gear excels for casting accuracy, because you can "thumb" the spool to stop the lure precisely where you want it. And a baitcasting outfit handles heavy monofilament and braided lines better than a spinning outfit. Baitcasting reels have a push button or thumb bar that frees the spool so you can cast without the reel handle turning. Although backlashing can be a problem because of the rotating spool, innovations such as magnetic anti-backlash devices have greatly reduced the problem. Baitcasting rods are generally stiffer and have smaller guides than spinning rods.

TROLLING. These outfits provide the line capacity needed for downrigger or longline trolling with heavy line. The large, rugged level-wind reels usually have smooth star drags. Trolling rods vary from long and limber, for downrigger trolling, to short and stiff, for trolling with big plugs.

FLYCASTING. A fly rod is designed to cast a thick fly line, which in turn pulls along a 7- to 10-foot monofilament leader and a fly. The long rod, usually measuring 7 1/2 to 9 feet, flexes over its entire length to help pick up and propel the fly line. The fly reel has no function in casting; it serves mainly to store line and fight fish.

WHAT TO LOOK FOR IN A FISHING ROD

Selecting the best rod for a particular type of fishing can be a highly confusing task. Besides the basic considerations – length, power and action – anglers should also pay attention to rod sensitivity. The explanations that follow will simplify the rod-selection process.

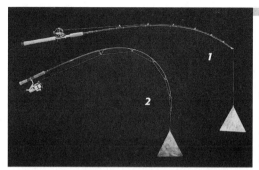

POWER, or strength, is demonstrated by lifting equal weights with a (1) heavy-power rod and a (2) light-power rod of the same length. Notice that the heavy-power rod flexes much less.

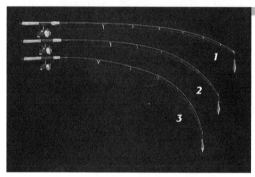

ACTION is demonstrated by lifting equal weights with different rods of the same power. A (1) fast-action rod bends mainly near the tip; a (2) medium-action, over the front half; and a (3) slow-action, over the entire length.

LENGTH. A long rod is generally better for distance casting and controlling the lure, but a short rod may be needed in tight quarters. In the past, short rods were needed to achieve the desired degree of stiffness, but with the space-age materials now available, it's possible to achieve the same stiffness in a longer fishing rod. As a result, the trend is toward increasing rod length.

POWER. A rod's power is the amount of force required to bend it. Some manufacturers rate power only as light, medium, heavy, medium-heavy, etc., while others use a numerical 1 to 10 system, with 1 being the lightest. The heavier the lure and the larger the fish, the more powerful the rod you'll need.

Light rods bend backward, or *load*, under the weight of a light lure. The force generated by the rod whipping forward makes casting easier. Heavy rods are needed for heavy lures. A light rod would not have the power to whip the lure forward or to sink the hooks into a big fish's jaws.

Obstacles such as thick weedbeds or timber make it necessary to use a heavy rod, so you can stop a fish's run and keep it away from snags.

ACTION. The action of a rod refers to where it bends. Action, which is primarily determined by degree of taper of the rod shaft, is usually rated as slow, medium, fast, extra-fast, etc.

Fast-action rods are the best choice when you need a responsive tip for twitching a surface lure or detecting subtle strikes when jigging. A fast tip also gives you a quicker, stronger hook-set. Medium-action rods are ideal for live-bait fishing, because the fish is less likely to feel resistance from the soft tip and drop the bait. Slow-action rods work like a shock absorber, cushioning the fight of a big fish so it won't break the line.

Perhaps the biggest factor confusing the rod-selection process is misuse of the terms *power* and *action* among salesclerks, writers and even some manufacturers. They commonly refer to a light-action rod, for instance, when they really mean light-power. Before buying a rod, make sure the salesperson understands these terms.

SENSITIVITY. A rod's sensitivity is the ability it has to telegraph vibrations from the line down the rod and on to the hand. Sensitivity is determined by the material the rod is made of, the rod's action and the physical weight of the rod.

A graphite rod, for example, transmits vibrations better than a fiberglass rod. When comparing two rods made from the same material, the rod with the fastest action is usually the most sensitive. And finally, when comparing two rods of the same material with identical actions, the rod that weighs the least will be the most sensitive.

> SENSITIVITY can be tested by attaching a reel to the rod and tying an 8- to 10-inch piece of stiff monofilament line to the rod tip. Hold the rod as you normally would when working a lure. Close your eyes, and have someone flick the hanging section of line with a finger. You should feel the vibration through a sensitive fishing rod.

32

WHAT TO LOOK FOR IN
A FISHING REEL

Selecting the right reel for your style of fishing can be confusing. When you walk into a tackle shop, you'll often see a display with dozens of similar-looking reels that vary greatly in price. The most expensive models may have features such as "infinite anti-reverse," which mean nothing to the average angler.

For the best performance from any kind of fishing outfit, the reel must be balanced with the rod. If you use a reel that weighs too much for the rod, the outfit will feel butt-heavy. Not only will you have problems casting, the heavy butt will take away from the sensitivity of the tip. Conversely, a reel that is too light for the rod will make the outfit feel tip-heavy, and your wrist will soon tire from trying to hold the rod up.

TYPES OF REELS

SPINNING. The spool of a spinning reel does not turn when you cast; the line simply flows off the end of the spool once the *bail* is opened. Reels come with either manual bails or bail triggers, which allow you to open the bail using one hand.

A spinning reel with a front drag is smoother and more reliable than one with a rear drag. A front drag employs washers that press on a large, flat surface, much like disk brakes on a car. A rear drag applies pressure on a small-diameter drive shaft, explaining why the drag may seem jerky. Some fishermen, however, prefer rear-drag reels because the drag is easier to adjust while fighting a fish.

SPINCASTING. A favorite among beginning anglers, these inexpensive reels are much like spinning reels, except the spool is covered to minimize tangling problems. The push-button style is used with a baitcasting rod; the underspin style, with a spinning rod. When selecting a spincasting reel, look for one with a smooth drag. The most inexpensive models often have sticky drags, resulting in many broken lines.

BAITCASTING. Used primarily for fishing with heavier lines and lures, baitcasting reels have smooth, dependable drag systems designed to handle big fish. Round reels hold the most line and have either a thumb-bar spool release or a push-button spool release. Low-profile reels feature a thumb-bar spool release and are more comfortable to *palm* during the retrieve. Modern baitcasting reels feature spool-braking systems that almost totally eliminate backlashes.

TROLLING. These large-capacity, level-wind reels are used mainly for longline trolling. They may hold several hundred yards of 20- to 30-pound monofilament. Because they do not have an anti-backlash mechanism, they should not be used for casting. Some trolling reels have a digital line counter that enables you to return your lure to the precise depth should you catch a fish.

FLY FISHING. The primary function of the fly reel is to hold the fly line while casting. However, some of the more sophisticated fly reels feature adjustable disc-drag systems, which help fight powerful fish such as steelhead and striped bass. Most fly reels have an exposed spool rim that allows you to apply additional drag tension by pressing the palm of your open hand against the rim.

Lines & Knots

The age of synthetics has given anglers a wider choice of lines than ever before. It's important to select the line best suited to the fishing conditions.

LINE TYPES

MONOFILAMENT LINES. Used in both spinning and baitcasting, mono is inexpensive, easy to cast and nearly invisible in water. Its major drawback is its high stretch factor.

You can select from many types and colors of mono. Plastic-worm or jig fishermen, who detect strikes by watching for a line twitch, may favor fluorescent mono when fishing discolored water but would probably use clear or green mono in clearer water. Anglers who fish rocky bottoms prefer abrasion-resistant mono. Live-bait fishermen use thin, flexible mono for a natural presentation. Don't buy cheap, off-brand mono. It weakens quickly, tends to be very kinky and may have thin spots. Abrasion, sunlight and airborne chemicals deteriorate line, so it pays to replace it regularly.

BRAIDED LINES. Braided lines have little stretch, so they work well for telegraphing bites and getting strong hook-sets. In the past, nylon and Dacron® were the only choices in braided-line materials. But today, fishermen can opt for space-age fibers, such as Spectra® and Kevlar®, which have even less stretch and a much thinner diameter for their strength. Modern braided lines are three to four times as strong as mono of equal diameter.

Nylon and Dacron lines, because of their thick diameter, are used primarily on baitcasting reels and for backing on fly reels. Modern braided lines, however, work equally well with spinning gear.

FLY LINES. *Level* lines have the same diameter over their entire length. Although they are inexpensive, level lines are hard to cast. *Double-taper* lines, with a level middle section and gradual tapers at each end, allow a delicate presentation. When one end wears out, the line can be reversed for economy. *Weight-forward* lines have a short, thick belly behind the tapered front end; the rear portion is tapered to a long, thin section, called *running line.* The up-front weight makes it easier to punch into a strong wind and make longer casts. *Shooting-head* lines are similar to weight-forward lines, but the weight forward section is much more compact. They cast farther than other lines.

Most fly lines float, but full-sinking or sink-tip types are available. Most shooting-head lines sink. Line weight designations range from 1 (lightest) to 12 (heaviest). For best casting performance, the line must be matched to the weight designation on the rod.

WIRE LINES. Single-strand and braided-wire lines, used mainly for deep-trolling or jigging, have no stretch, but kink easily. Some braided-wire lines are coated with plastic to reduce kinkiness. Wire lines are also used to make leaders for toothy gamefish, such as northern pike and muskies.

Lead-core lines, commonly used for deep-trolling, are more flexible than other wire lines, but their thick diameter requires a large reel. Most lead-core is color-coded so you can easily monitor your fishing depth.

KNOTS

Your fishing line is only as strong as the knots used in tying it. All knots weaken line to some degree, and some knots cut line strength in half.

The knots on the following pages are good choices for the purposes described, though many other knots can be substituted. As a rule, avoid any knots that put sharp bends in your line, because those bends may fracture under stress.

The ability to tie good knots will save you from losing countless lures and fish. Below are some important knot-tying tips:

•*Choose knots* that are easy to tie; even the strongest knot will fail if not tied properly.

•*All knots weaken* with use. Get in the habit of tying new knots before every trip, and retie knots frequently.

•*Moisten the knot* before snugging it up. This reduces the friction that can cause slight abrasions when you pull the knot tight.

•*Snug up the knot* with a smooth, strong pull. Do not be timid about testing it. Better it should break while being tied than after hooking a big fish.

•*Leave a little extra line* when clipping the tag end. Some knots slip slightly just before they break, and the extra line is good insurance.

•*Tie knots carefully.* A slight scratch from a nail clipper is barely visible to the naked eye, but it will greatly reduce the line's strength.

•*Retie* should an overhand knot accidentally form in your line or leader. An overhand knot has a very sharp bend, and will usually cause the line to fail at about 50 percent of its rated strength.

LINE TO SPOOL: ARBOR KNOT, STRENGTH 60%

LOOP THE LINE around the spool, then tie (top) an overhand knot around the standing line to form a loose slip knot. Tie an overhand knot in the free end and snug it up. Pull firmly on the standing line until the knot in the free end snugs up against the slip knot (bottom). The arbor knot will not slip when you wind line onto the spool.

HOOK TO LINE:
TRILENE KNOT, STRENGTH 90%

PASS (1) THE LINE through the eye of the hook twice from the same side, leaving a double loop next to the eye. (2) Wrap the free end around the standing line about 5 times. (3) Push the free end of the line through the double loop. (4) Moisten the line and snug up the knot with a firm pull on the line and hook; trim. The Trilene knot is an excellent knot because it ties easily, stacks smoothly and has no sharp bends. It is also one of the strongest fishing knots, with a rating of 90 percent of line strength.

LOOP IN LINE OR LEADER:
DOUBLE SURGEON'S LOOP, STRENGTH 70%

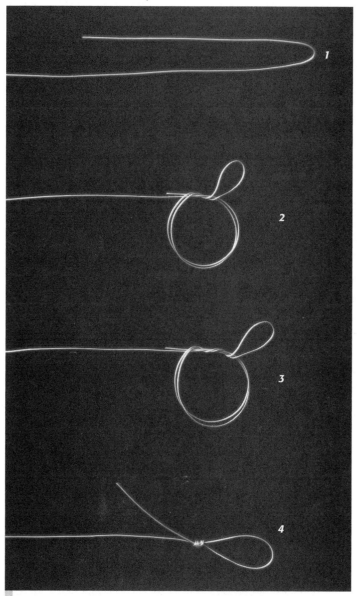

DOUBLE UP (1) the last 6 inches of the line. (2) Make a loose over-hand knot in double line. (3) Pass loop end through knot a second time to form double overhand knot. (4) Tighten by holding loop while pulling standing line and tag end until snug. Trim tag.

LURE TO LOOP:
DUNCAN LOOP, STRENGTH 90%

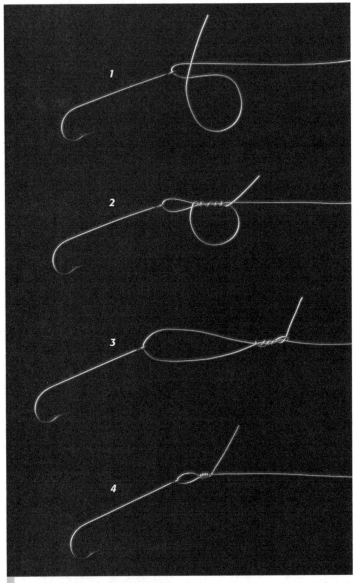

PASS (1) END OF LINE through hook. Form a loop in tag end, as shown.
(2) Pass tag end through loop. Wind tag end through loop and around
standing line 4 times, winding away from hook. (3) Pull tag end to snug
up knot. (4) Slide knot to desired position by pulling on standing line.
Trim tag.

SPLICING LINES OF SIMILAR DIAMETER:
BLOOD KNOT, STRENGTH 65%

SPLICING LINES OF SIMILAR DIAMETER: BLOOD KNOT, STRENGTH 65%

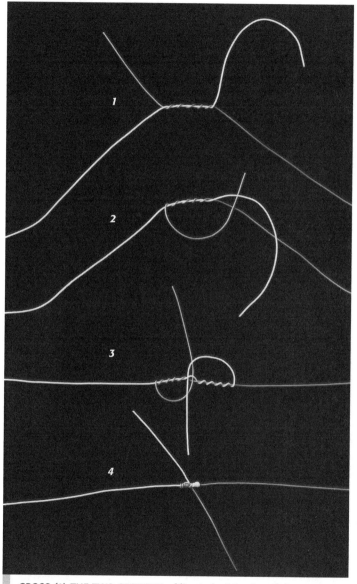

CROSS (1) THE TWO SECTIONS of line to be joined, and then wrap one tag end around standing part of other line 5 to 7 times, depending on line diameter. (2) Pass tag end back between the two lines. (3) Wrap other tag end in the same manner, and bring it back through the same opening. (4) Pull standing lines to tighten knot; trim.

SPLICING LINES OF DIFFERENT DIAMETERS OR MATERIALS: DOUBLE SURGEON'S KNOT, STRENGTH 100%

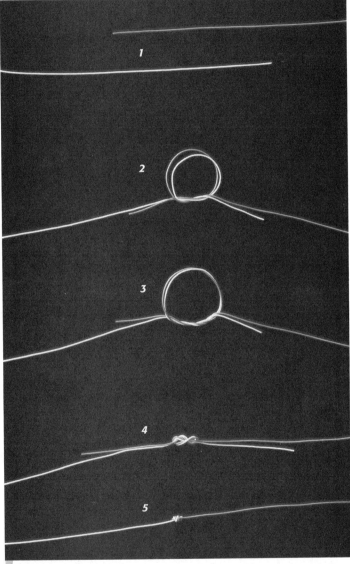

PLACE (1) TWO SECTIONS of line to be joined side by side, tag ends facing opposite directions. (2) Make a loop in double line. Pass both ends of line on right through loop to form an overhand knot. (3) Pass same ends through loop a second time to form double overhand knot. (4) Tighten knot by pulling all four ends slowly and evenly. (5) Trim tag ends close to knot.

LEADER BUTT TO FLY LINE:
TUBE KNOT

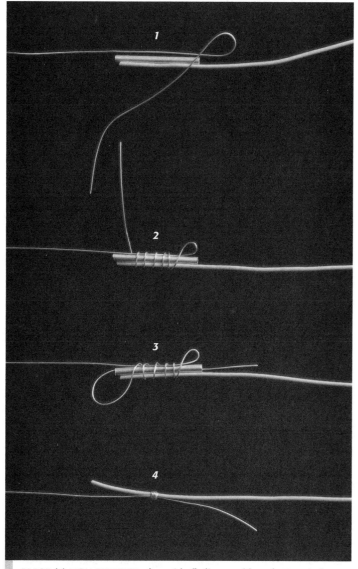

PLACE (1) HOLLOW TUBE alongside fly line, and loop butt end of
leader alongside tube, as shown. (2) Wrap butt end around tube, fly
line and standing part of leader 5 to 6 times. (3) Pass butt through
tube, remove tube and pull on tag end and standing part of leader
until knot is snug. (4) Tighten knot slowly, using your fingernails to
position wraps; trim closely.

Casting
Techniques

In casting, the two main considerations are distance and accuracy. As a rule, spinning gear gives you better distance; baitcasting gear, better accuracy.

The secret to becoming a proficient caster is learning to let the rod do the work. If you try to throw the lure rather than let the spring of the rod flick it out, you'll lose both distance and accuracy.

Your rod's power, action, length, weight, guide size and guide placement greatly affect casting performance. If the rod is too powerful for the weight of the lure, it will not load enough on the backcast, and you'll have no choice but to throw the lure. If the rod is too light for the lure, it won't have enough power to propel the lure.

The lighter the lure, the more important it is to use a slow-action rod so the entire rod contributes casting power. The longer the rod, the more leverage for longer casts. Guides that are too small restrict line flow and create friction, which reduces casting distance. If the guides are spaced too far apart, the line slaps the rod between the guides during the cast, also causing excess friction.

The type and weight of your line also affect casting. The stiffer and heavier the line, the shorter your casts. Don't use line heavier than needed for the conditions. Be sure to fill the spool, but don't overfill it.

You can make long, accurate casts with most any modern reel, although there are a few specific considerations. Long-spool spinning reels, for instance, cast farther than those with shorter spools because the line level decreases very little from the start of the cast to the finish. When you try to make a long cast with a short-spool, narrow-arbor reel, the line begins slapping the spool toward the end of the cast, reducing casting distance.

How to Cast Spinning, Baitcasting & Flyfishing Gear

SPINNING GEAR

1. HOLD the line with your index finger to prevent line from flowing off the spool with the bail open.

2. BRING the rod back briskly, stopping at the 10 o'clock position. The rod should bend back, or load, from the weight of the lure.

3. STROKE the rod forward with a smooth wrist motion, and, midway through the forward stroke, release the line from your index finger.

4. FEATHER the line with your index finger to stop the lure precisely on the target.

BAITCASTING GEAR

1. PRESS the spool release and thumb the spool to prevent line from spinning off prematurely.

2. BRING the rod back briskly, stopping at the 10 o'clock position, just as you do in spincasting. For best accuracy, use a straight overhand motion.

3. STROKE the rod forward with a smooth wrist motion, and, midway through the forward stroke, lift your thumb to release the line.

4. THUMB the spool as needed during the cast to minimize backlashing and to stop the lure exactly where you want it.

FLYFISHING GEAR

1. LET OUT the amount of line you want to cast in front of you. Stand facing your target with feet spread comfortably apart. Position your rod hand so the tip of the rod is pointing in the direction of the target, with rod, forearm and wrist aligned. Lower your rod tip and remove the slack from the line.

2. RAISE your rod and begin to accelerate slowly and continuously until the entire fly line is off the water.

3. APPLY a short, backward speed stroke, forcing a bend in the rod and propelling the line into the backcast.

4. STOP the rod crisply. A loop will form in the line as it moves overhead.

5. PAUSE as the backcast unrolls behind you. When the line forms a small "J," begin your forward acceleration.

6. MAKE a short, fast forward stroke and immediately stop the rod. Aim your cast about eye level above your target. Let the line settle to the water, while lowering the rod tip to the fishing position.

Terminal Tackle

You can spend a small fortune on a boat equipped with all the modern electronics and outfit yourself with the best rods and reels, but if you don't have the right terminal tackle, you won't catch as many fish as you should.

Novice anglers often make the mistake of overrigging – using terminal tackle that is too heavy for the type of fishing they're doing – because they don't want to risk losing a fish to a bent hook or snap. But heavy terminal tackle makes your bait look unnatural and interferes with its action, so you get fewer bites. The best policy is to select the lightest terminal tackle suitable for the conditions.

A finicky walleye, for instance, may turn up its nose at a nightcrawler rigged on a size 2 hook attached to a snap-swivel. But it will eagerly suck in the same worm rigged on a size 6 short-shank hook tied directly to monofilament line.

In some situations, however, delicacy is not an issue. An aggressive pike or muskie will take a foot-long baitfish rigged on the biggest hook attached to the heaviest snap, and will swim leisurely away with the bait, towing a float the size of a tennis ball.

Following are guidelines for choosing the basic types of terminal tackle.

FLOATS. Popular types of floats include: *slip-bobber,* for fishing live bait in deep water; *lighted float,* for night fishing; *cylinder float,* for slip-bobber fishing with large baits; *clip-on float,* the most common and inexpensive type; *removable slip-bobber,* which can be added to your line after the rest of the rig has been tied; *peg-bobber,* for delicate shallow-water presentations; *casting bubble,* for casting flies or other nearly weightless lures; *weighted casting float,* for reaching distant targets; and *spring-lock float,* which attaches easily.

SINKERS. Popular sinker styles
include: *keel,* to prevent line twist when
trolling; *pyramid,* for holding heavy baits in fast current;
bell, a general-purpose weight; *Snap-Loc*® and *Rubber-cor*®,
which can easily be added to or removed from your line;
egg and *walking,* for slip-sinker fishing; *bullet,* for fishing in
weedy cover; *split-shot* and *pinch-on,* for precisely weighting
your bait; *Baitwalker*® and *bottom bouncer,* for deep-trolling
with a minimum of snags.

HOOKS. Popular hook styles include: *short-shank hook,*
used for most live-bait fishing; *long-shank hook,* which can
be easily removed from sunfish and other species that
swallow the hook; *egg hook,* for burying in salmon eggs;
sliced-shank hook, for keeping worms and other bait from
sliding down the shank; *weedless hook,* for fishing in heavy
cover; *worm hook,* used for Texas-rigging (p. 75) soft plastics; *Siwash*® *hook,* used on spoons and other artificials,
with long point for easy penetration; and *treble hook,* used
on many artificials and for holding moldable stinkbaits.

ATTACHMENT DEVICES. Common devices for attaching lures or hooks and joining lines include: *snap-swivel,*
used for attaching lures that could twist your line; *Cross-
Lok*® *snap,* for attaching lures that will not twist your line;
barrel swivel, used for connecting line and leader or splicing
into line to eliminate twist; *quick snaps,* for attaching small
lures; *split-rings,* used for attaching hooks to lure, or line to
lure; *metal leader,* for preventing bite-offs from toothy fish
such as northern pike.

Fishing Boats

A good fishing boat must be designed for the type of waters you fish, and it should be laid out and rigged for your style of fishing. A jon boat, for instance, may be ideal for fishing a small river, but its low profile makes it unsafe for use on a large lake. A bass boat (above) is perfect for casting, but the transom is too low for backtrolling on a windy day. Console steering offers comfort, easy steering and good visibility while speeding from spot to spot, but tiller steering gives you better boat control for trolling.

Boats with flat, open floors and comfortable swivel seats allow anglers to move about easily while casting or fighting a fish.

Modern boats are commonly rigged with many sophisticated accessories. Besides depth finders and other electronics, they're often equipped with front and rear trolling motors, live wells, bilge pumps, anchor winches, spotlights, on-board chargers and even such luxury items as AM-FM marine-band cassette players.

Following are descriptions of the most popular types of fishing boats used by freshwater anglers:

BASS BOAT. The ultimate in speed and fishing comfort, these luxurious boats are often rigged with 150- to 200-hp outboards and can reach speeds exceeding 70 mph.

DEEP-V. Often called *walleye boats*, these boats are ideal for fishing large, windswept lakes. Console- or tiller-operated, many of these boats are rigged with small-horsepower "kicker" motors for trolling.

SEMI-V. These 12- to 16-foot boats are inexpensive, yet versatile. Larger, deeper models are used on big lakes, while smaller ones are often used as "car-toppers" to fish waters with poor access.

JON BOAT. Rugged and stable, yet inexpensive, the jon boat has a very shallow draft, making it an excellent choice for shallow, stumpy backwaters, marshy lakes and rock-strewn rivers.

CANOE. Light and easy to paddle, a canoe allows you to fish small lakes, ponds and rivers where access is difficult. Small outboards can be used on square-stern canoes or standard canoes with a motor bracket.

FLOAT TUBE AND KICK BOAT. These small one-person watercraft are lightweight, easily transported and ideal for exploring small bodies of water with poor access. Most float tubes and kick boats are propelled using kick fins or oars.

Sonar Devices & Other Electronics

Before the age of electronic fishing, anglers had only a vague idea of water depth and bottom contour. And if they found a hot spot in a large body of water, they would have to be lucky to find it a second time.

Today, many anglers use navigational tools (p. 56), such as Loran (long-range navigation) and GPS (global positioning system) to return unerringly to their spots, and once they get there, they check the depth and scout for fish with sophisticated sonar units.

Modern anglers also rely on other electronic aids, such as temperature gauges, trolling speed indicators and marine radios. Together, these electronics take much of the guesswork out of the sport, enabling anglers to catch fish more consistently.

SONAR DEVICES. Commonly called depth finders or fish locators, sonar devices come in four basic types: liquid-crystal recorders (LCRs), video graphs, flashers and paper graphs, which have been almost completely replaced by the other three.

All sonar devices operate on the same principle. The transducer, which can be attached to the boat's hull, transom or trolling motor, sends sound waves to the bottom, and the returning echos are recorded on a screen or, in the case of a flasher, displayed instantly on a dial. The screen or dial displays the bottom and any other objects above it, such as fish or weeds. With a little experience, the operator can also learn to distinguish different bottom types (p. 53).

When selecting a sonar unit, consider the cone angle of the transducer, which determines how much of the bottom the sonar signal covers. A narrow cone (20 degrees or less) is best for detecting bottom-hugging fish because it has a thinner "blind spot" (p. 55) than a wide-cone transducer. A wider cone is better for vertically jigging or downrigger trolling for suspended fish, because you can monitor a larger area and see the depth of your lure or cannonball.

OTHER ELECTRONIC AIDS. Fish often concentrate in specific temperature layers, around colder or warmer tributaries or in bays that are warmer than other parts of a lake. Temperature gauges help you locate these zones quickly. Some gauges monitor only surface temperature while others come with long cords that allow you to take the temperature at any depth.

Another electronic aid used by many fishermen is the trolling-speed indicator, which allows you to precisely monitor how fast you're trolling, so you can maintain the speed that fish prefer. And gaining in popularity are marine radios. They make it possible to exchange information with anglers several miles away. Most marine radios have weather bands to keep you informed of approaching storms.

Of all electronic aids, however, sonar devices are without question the most important to your fishing success. Perhaps the greatest difference between the expert and average angler lies in the expert's ability to accurately interpret the signals seen on the depth finder. The following pages explain the basic types of depth finders and provide tips for using them correctly.

BASIC TYPES OF DEPTH FINDERS

LIQUID-CRYSTAL RECORDERS (right) display the sonar signal on a screen made up of tiny squares, or *pixels*. For good resolution, the vertical pixel count should be at least 128. Some LCRs can be linked to GPS modules, which turn the sonar device into a GPS navigation instrument.

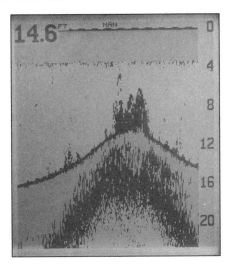

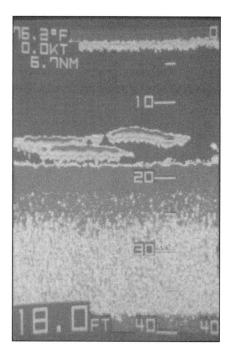

VIDEO GRAPHS (left) display the sonar signal on a cathode-ray tube, much like a television set. Videos are bulky, but give you better resolution than an LCR. Some video graphs have a color display, with different colors representing different-sized targets.

FLASHERS (below) show the sonar signal on a calibrated dial or bar display. Unlike other sonar devices, flashers give you an instantaneous readout of targets, even at speeds over 60 mph. For this reason, flashers are the favorite sonar device for many expert fishermen.

PAPER GRAPHS display the sonar signal on paper, giving you a permanent record of your fishing day. While paper graphs provide excellent resolution, they have lost popularity, due to the inconvenience and expense of having to replace the paper.

HOW TO INTERPRET GRAPH READINGS

HARD BOTTOM is indicated by a thick gray band (left bracket); soft bottom, a thin gray band (right bracket).

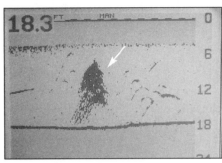

BAITFISH SCHOOLS (arrow) appear as an irregular clump not connected to the bottom.

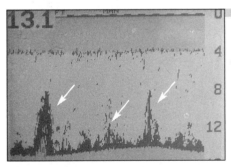

WEEDS (arrows) appear as irregular shapes projecting off the bottom.

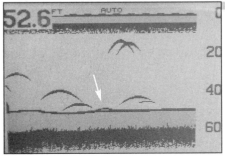

BOTTOM-HUGGING FISH (arrow) can be distinguished from the bottom by "air" beneath the signal.

UNDERSTANDING "HOOK SIZE" ON A GRAPH

Many fishermen think a big hook on their paper graph, LCR or video means a big fish. It could be, but it could also mean a small fish. Here's why.

Suppose two fish of equal size swim underneath your stationary boat. The first fish (number 1 in example A) is only a few feet down, where the cone is narrow. As a result, it passes through the cone quickly and makes only a short mark. The second fish (2) swims near the bottom, where the cone is wide. It spends more time in the cone, and consequently makes a much longer mark.

EXAMPLE A

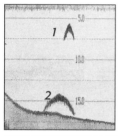

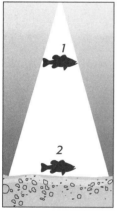

Here's another example: You're drifting or slow-trolling and pass over a bluegill (number 3 in example B) that is motionless or swimming slowly with the boat. It makes a long mark because it stays in the cone until the boat moves away. Then a good-sized bass (4) swims rapidly through the cone. It makes a shorter mark because it passes through the cone more quickly.

EXAMPLE B

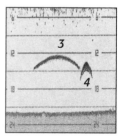

A more reliable indicator of fish size than arc length is arc thickness. The thickness depends on the strength of the reflected signal. And big fish reflect a much stronger signal than do little fish.

UNDERSTANDING A DEPTH FINDER'S BLIND SPOT

It's a mistake to fish only where you "see" fish with your graph, flasher, LCR or video. These devices have a blind spot or "dead zone" – an area in the sound cone where a depth finder cannot display any targets. The dead zone is thickest at the edge of the cone and thinnest directly beneath the transducer. If fish are in this zone, you won't see them.

The thickness of the blind spot directly beneath the transducer is determined by your sonar device's target separation, which is the depth finder's ability to distinguish and display targets that are close together vertically. These targets could be fish, weeds or the bottom.

For example, if your sonar device has a target separation of 3 inches, and two small perch swim through the sound cone one on top of the other, the locator will display them as a single target. However, if the two fish separate so one is swimming 4 inches higher than the other, the sonar will display them as two targets. In other words, if your sonar has a target separation of 3 inches, the blind spot directly beneath the transducer is 3 inches thick.

To understand why the blind spot is thickest at the edge of the cone, you must be familiar with how a sonar device displays the depth. For example, suppose the verticle distance from your transducer to the bottom measures 15 feet. The only objects that are seen on the locator's screen are those that are less than 15 feet away from the transducer. But a fish just off the bottom and on the edge of the cone is more than 15 feet away from the transducer and lost in the blind spot.

You can't eliminate the blind spot, but you can gain a better understanding of what's happening beneath the boat by determining how thick the zone for your depth finder really is. Drop a jig to the bottom. Lower the rod tip to the water and reel in any slack. Lift the rod tip until the jig appears on the depth finder, and note the distance between the water and rod tip. That distance is the thickness of your blind spot in that particular part of the sound cone and depth of water.

Maps & Navigation Equipment

Hydrographic maps, also called *contour maps,* are one of a fisherman's most valuable tools. They enable you to quickly find likely fish-holding structure that could otherwise be found only by hours of intensive scouting. Although hydrographic maps don't necessarily show every piece of structure in a given body of water, they reveal the largest, most prominent pieces. There will always be small points, inside turns and sunken islands that don't show up on the map.

In addition to hydrographic maps, fishermen often make use of other map types. *River charts,* for example, show locks and dams, submerged wingdams, riprap banks and mileage markers. *Reservoir maps* identify dams, stands of flooded timber, old roadbeds and the old river channel. *GPS maps* show the precise latitude and longitude of lake features, which enables anglers to motor directly to a desired spot. And *recreation maps* include information valuable to anglers, such as location of public access sites and a list of fish species that are present in a particular body of water.

Maps are available through a wide variety of sources, including private companies, state or provincial natural-resource agencies, the U.S. Army Corps of Engineers and the Bureau of Reclamation.

Once a luxury enjoyed mainly by big-water boaters, navigation equipment is rapidly gaining popularity on most types of fishing waters. Not only does it enable you to quickly find your spots, it makes fishing safer by helping you navigate accurately in the fog and at night.

Navigation equipment also makes it easier to share fishing information. Rather than try to explain the location of a hard-to-find spot over the phone, for instance, an angler can give a friend the exact navigation coordinates.

Loran-C navigators rely on signals from U.S. Coast Guard operated radio towers; GPS, on signals from U.S. military

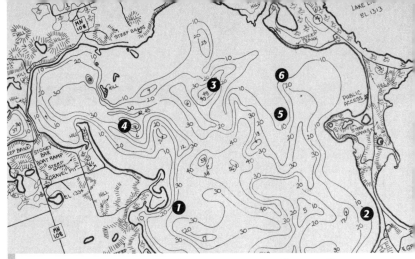

HYDROGRAPHIC MAPS show a body of water's structure with contour lines. (1) Closely spaced lines signify a sharp drop-off; (2) widely spaced lines, a gradual drop-off. Holes are indicated by (3) a series of concentric contour lines, with the greatest depth in the middle. Humps, or sunken islands, are also indicated by (4) a series of concentric contour lines, but the shallowest depth is in the middle. (5) Underwater points protrude out from the shore and (6) inside turns are shown by the sharp curve of the contour lines.

satellites. GPS is the superior system, because it can be used anywhere on Earth.

Many anglers are intimidated by the complexity of navigation devices, so they are hesitant to purchase one. One reason navigation devices seem so complex is that they have many advanced features that the average angler may never use. Most fishermen simply want to mark the location of a particular *waypoint*, such as a good fishing spot or a boat landing, so they can find it again later. The procedure for doing that, whether you're using a Loran or GPS unit, is quite simple.

After you use your navigation unit for awhile and become comfortable with it, you can begin experimenting with some of the more complex features, such as setting up a navigation route that leads you to a series of waypoints.

GPS has become far more popular than Loran. It is easier to operate, because you do not have to pre-program the unit to select certain signals. And it is more reliable, because it is not affected by weather. Another advantage: GPS units process navigation data more rapidly, usually within a second or two. Because the screen is updated so fast, there is less chance for steering error.

Trolling Equipment

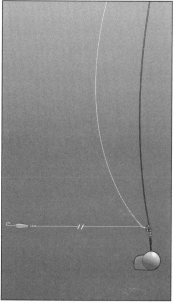

Trolling has always been one of the most effective techniques for catching fish. Perhaps no other method allows you to present one or more lures to large numbers of fish spread out over a vast area.

For many fishermen, trolling involves nothing more than making a long cast behind the boat and maintaining a trolling speed and water depth appropriate for their lure choice. But modern innovations in trolling gear have revolutionized this age-old fishing method.

TYPES OF TROLLING DEVICES

DOWNRIGGERS (left) enable you to fish in deep water with relatively light tackle. An 8- to 12-pound lead weight, or *cannonball,* is lowered to the desired depth on a stainless steel cable. The fishing line is then attached to a release that trips when a fish strikes, allowing you to play the fish on a free line. Anglers no longer have to guess how deep their lure is running or how fast it is going. They can set the downrigger to fish at a precise depth while a speed sensor can be attached to the downrigger cable to tell them exactly how fast the lure is moving at that depth. Some downriggers even feature bottom-tracking systems that raise and lower automatically to stay at a predetermined distance above the bottom. A transducer on the transom sends a signal to the downrigger, telling it when to change depth. Two or more downriggers can operate off the same sonar signal, all changing depths simultaneously.

SIDE PLANERS AND TROLLING BOARDS. With these devices, trollers are no longer limited to fishing straight behind the boat. By attaching their lines to side planers or trolling boards, they can reach fish that may have moved off to the side when the boat passed over them.

Side planers attach to your line and pull it to the side as the boat moves forward. A strike trips a release, and the planer slides down the line until it hits a stop several feet from the lure.

Trolling boards plane to the side on a separate cord, which is held by a planer mast. The fishing line is attached to the cord with a release. As the boat moves forward, the release slides down the cord to the desired point. A strike trips the release, and the angler fights the fish on a free line.

DIVING PLANES. This planing device goes down as well as out. This enables deepwater anglers to cover a much wider swath of water than they would using only downriggers. Diving planes, such as the Dipsey Diver®, track right, left or straight, depending on how you adjust the rudder. Tie your line to the front eye of the Dipsey Diver, and your lure to a 6- to 8-foot leader, which is attached to the rear eye. When a fish strikes, the diving plane flattens so you can reel in the fish without pulling against the plane.

3

BASIC
GAMEFISH
TECHNIQUES

Largemouth Bass

Anglers from Canada to Cuba have marveled at the explosive strike and breathtaking leaps of the largemouth bass. With its huge mouth open wide, a hooked largemouth takes to the air, shaking its head violently to throw the hook. Often it succeeds.

The largemouth has become the most widely distributed gamefish in North America, partly because of its reputation as a fighter, but primarily because of its remarkable ability to survive in almost any freshwater lake, pond or stream. It thrives in pine-fringed lakes of southern Canada, murky backwaters in Illinois and sprawling desert reservoirs in Mexico.

Black bass, bucketmouth and old linesides are but a few names for the largemouth bass, which is actually a member of the sunfish family. Like sunfish and crappies, bass fan out shallow, saucer-shaped nests in the spring, usually in water 2 to 4 feet deep. Most spawning grounds are in bays, cuts or channels protected from the wind. Rough water can easily scatter eggs or destroy nests on windward shores.

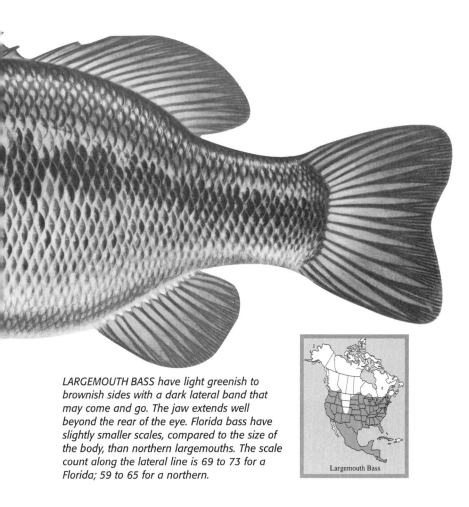

LARGEMOUTH BASS have light greenish to brownish sides with a dark lateral band that may come and go. The jaw extends well beyond the rear of the eye. Florida bass have slightly smaller scales, compared to the size of the body, than northern largemouths. The scale count along the lateral line is 69 to 73 for a Florida; 59 to 65 for a northern.

Largemouth Bass

Largemouth bass spawn when water warms to the low- to mid-60s. Bass in Florida usually deposit their eggs in February, while largemouths in Minnesota may not spawn until mid-June. After dropping her eggs, the female leaves the male to guard the eggs and the young until they can fend for themselves. Nest-guarding males may strike at almost anything that swims their way. This explains why some states close the bass season or prohibit angling in certain spawning areas until the nesting season is over.

Typical bass foods are small fish, crayfish, frogs and insect larvae. The largemouth can adapt to almost any type of fresh water, because it eats a wide variety of foods. Snakes, turtles, mice and even birds have been found in bass stomachs.

Largemouth bass shy away from bright sunlight and are most active under dim conditions. On sunny summer days, they feed at daybreak and dusk, spending midday along drop-offs close to feeding areas. Fishing is usually good on rainy or overcast days, but poor during and after a thunderstorm.

There are two subspecies of largemouth bass: the northern largemouth and the Florida largemouth. The two look nearly identical, but the Florida bass grows much faster. A trophy bass in Vermont might weigh 6 pounds, while 12-pound bass are not uncommon in Florida.

The world-record largemouth, 22 pounds, 4 ounces, was taken in Montgomery Lake, Georgia, in 1932. It is thought to be an intergrade between the two subspecies. Most experts believe the next world record will come from California, where several bass in the 20-pound class have been caught in recent years.

Where to Catch Largemouth Bass

Largemouth bass spend most of their lives in water that is only 5 to 15 feet deep, but they will sometimes move into deep water to find food or to escape sunlight. Bass in the shallows are likely to hold near some kind of shady cover, especially if that cover is near deep water.

Natural and man-made features that attract largemouth vary greatly depending on the type of water. In general, however, fishermen should begin to look for largemouths around the following: emergent vegetation, such as bulrushes; floating-leaved vegetation, such as lily pads; submerged weeds, such as coontail; overhanging trees; stumps; brush; bridge pilings and boat docks.

The time of the year that bass are found on certain structure and cover types also varies. Following is a list of prime bass locations in natural and man-made lakes throughout the season.

PRIME LOCATIONS IN NATURAL LAKES

•*Shallow bays* warm faster than the rest of the lake. Bass move in to feed and, later, spawn. Mud-bottomed bays warm first; the dark bottom absorbs the sun's rays.

•*Weedlines* hold bass in summer and fall. Outside weedlines form where the water becomes too deep for adequate light penetration. Inside weedlines may also form from wave action or the water freezing to the bottom.

•*Slop bays* hold bass in summer because the thick layer of floating weeds keeps the water below relatively cool. These bays also furnish an abundant supply of food.

•*Humps* with a weedy or rocky bottom make excellent summertime bass hangouts. The weeds and rocks offer shade and the bass can easily retreat into the adjacent deep water.

•*Points and inside turns* along the breakline hold bass from early summer through winter. Gradually sloping structure is best in summer; sharp-sloping in late fall and winter.

•*Shallow flats* draw bass on warm, sunny days in late fall and winter. Shallow flats along protected shores are best, because they warm the fastest.

PRIME LOCATIONS IN MAN-MADE LAKES

•*Main-lake points,* particularly the ones near the old river channel, concentrate bass in summer and winter. Bass move up on the points to feed and rest in the adjacent deep water.

•*River channel bends and intersections* hold more bass in summer than straight sections of channel. Because the deep water in the river channel stays relatively warm in winter, it often holds large numbers of bass.

•*Back ends of shallow creek arms,* especially those with no flow, have the warmest water in spring. Like bays in natural lakes, they draw bass to feed and spawn. They also draw bass in fall, because they are the first spots to cool.

•*Man-made features*, such as submerged roadbeds, railroad grades, riprap banks and old building foundations, are important bass structure throughout the year. Reservoir maps help you pinpoint these features.

•*Humps* with timber or weeds are prime summertime bass spots, especially if they are located near the main river channel.

•*Timbered flats* are top feeding areas from spring to fall. The best flats are usually along a creek channel or river channel, where bass have easy access to deeper water.

How to Catch Largemouth

Because largemouth bass eat most any kind of food and live in most any kind of water, bass anglers must learn to be versatile. If you rely on only one method, such as topwater fishing, you may have excellent success in some situations, but practically none in others. You must adjust your tactics depending on time of year, type of water, type of forage and type of cover.

For instance, topwater lures are dynamite on warm summer mornings and evenings, when bass are gorging themselves in the shallows. But fishing topwaters would probably be a waste of time on a cold morning in late fall, when the fish are not nearly as active.

In very clear water, topwaters work best in low-light periods, but in murky water, they will catch bass all day long. Water clarity also affects your choice of lure color. Bright or fluorescent colors are a good choice in discolored water, while natural colors that mimic bass foods are almost always more effective in very clear water.

When bass are roaming open water in search of pelagic baitfish, such as gizzard shad, lures like crankbaits and spinnerbaits that run in the mid-depths will usually outproduce bottom-bouncing lures, like jigs and Texas-rigged plastic worms.

Perhaps the most important consideration in lure selection

POLARIZED SUNGLASSES are a must for fishing largemouth bass and other species of fish that relate to shallow-water cover. With an unpolarized view (inset), the glare on the surface of the water prevents you from seeing fish and other underwater objects. However, the same scene viewed through a polarized lens reveals a largemouth (arrow) next to some rocks.

is cover type. If you're fishing in dense weeds or brush, for example, you need a lure that will track through the cover without continually fouling or snagging. Good choices include Texas-rigged worms, weedless jigs and spinnerbaits. In snag-free water, however, lures with open hooks work better because you'll hook a larger percentage of the fish that strike.

Lure selection is an important part of bass fishing, but it means very little unless you're familiar with the seasonal movement pattern of the fish on the particular body of water you're fishing. Until you discover this pattern, it pays to spend more time exploring the lake than cruising the aisles at the tackle store. If you can't find the fish, you can't catch them.

FISHING SPINNERBAITS

Spinnerbaits are the best all-season lures for largemouth bass. They are especially effective in spring, when bass are in weedy shallows. Because of their safety-pin design, most are virtually snagless; the bent shaft runs interference for the upturned hook.

As a result, you can toss a spinnerbait into dense weedbeds, brush or timber without constantly hanging up. Spinnerbaits can also be counted down to fish along drop-offs, jigged along the bottom in water as deep as 20 feet and even run on the surface with the blade nearly breaking water. Most anglers use 1/4- to 1-ounce spinnerbaits for largemouth.

Spinnerbaits come in two basic designs: *single-spins,* which have only one blade, and *tandem-spins,* which have two. A single-spin helicopters better, while a tandem-spin has more lift, making it a better choice for shallow-water presentations.

The style of blades on your spinnerbait also makes a difference. Colorado blades, for instance, have more water resistance than willow-leaf blades, so they spin better on a slow retrieve and ride higher in the water. Willow-leaf blades can be retrieved faster, so they work better for locating bass.

FISHING SUBSURFACE PLUGS

This lure category includes a variety of hard-bodied baits that run from a few feet to as much as 30 feet beneath the surface.

Designed to be retrieved quite rapidly, these lures have a built-in wobble that makes them resemble swimming baitfish.

Most plugs used for largemouth are 3 to 6 inches in length. They include 4 major types:

QUICK TIP: Bump the bottom with your plug or allow it to hit submerged branches and broad-leaved vegetation. This will change its action and may trigger strikes from bass.

MINNOW PLUGS. These long, thin-bodied lures have a small lip that gives them a tight wiggle. Some minnow plugs and crankbaits have long lips that make them run deep.

VIBRATING PLUGS. With the attachment eye on the

FISHING A SPINNERBAIT

BULGING. With your rod tip high, reel fast enough so that the blades almost, but not quite, break the surface and create a bulge. This retrieve will often draw bass up out of dense weedy or brushy cover.

SLOW-ROLLING. When bass are buried in heavy cover and not particularly active, try reeling a spinnerbait slowly, bumping into weeds, branches and other objects. The change in action of the blades may trigger strikes.

HELICOPTERING. When bass are holding tight to vertical cover, like flooded trees, reel a single-spin spinnerbait up to the cover and let it sink vertically. As it sinks, the blades will spin, drawing the attention of bass.

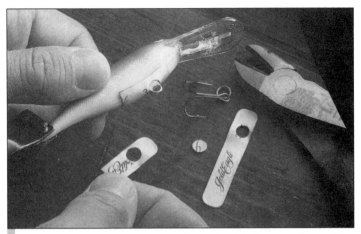

WEIGHT A SUBSURFACE PLUG to achieve the right buoyancy by applying strips of golfer's tape to the bottom. Seal in the tape with epoxy glue.

back, these sinking plugs have tight vibrating action that fish can detect even in low-clarity water.

CRANKBAITS. A plastic or metal lip creates the wobble in these lures. Most crankbaits have a short, aerodynamic body.

TROLLING PLUGS. These hard-to-cast plugs are a good choice for covering expanses of water. Most have flattened foreheads that give them a wide, enticing wobble.

TOPWATER FISHING

Topwaters create a disturbance on the surface that bass mistake for a mouse, large insect or struggling baitfish.

There are 6 important types of topwater lures:

STICKBAITS. These lures have no action of their own, but a twitching retrieve, called *walking-the-dog*, makes them dart from side to side.

> QUICK TIP:
> Wait until you feel the fish before setting the hook. If you attempt to set as soon as you see a splash, you'll probably miss the fish.

CHUGGERS. A scooped-out or flattened face makes these lures produce a chugging sound when you give them a sharp twitch.

CRAWLERS. A wide, cupped faceplate or collapsible arms

TIE YOUR LINE directly to the lure, rather than use a heavy clip or snap-swivel. The extra weight pulls the nose under, ruining the action.

give these lures the crawling action.

PROPBAIT. Propellers on one or both ends throw water when you reel rapidly. The baits can also be fished with a twitch-and-pause retrieve.

FROGS & RATS. Soft rubber or plastic-bodied frogs and rats have weedless hooks and can be retrieved over thick slop without fouling.

BUZZBAITS. The spinning buzzblade creates a lot of surface disturbance, and the safety-pin design makes these baits quite weedless.

JIGGING

These lures are ideal for pinpoint presentations to bass holding in tight spots. Although jigs and jigging lures work best in cool or cold water, they will catch bass most anytime.

JIGS. Lead-head jigs, usually called *bass jigs,* can be dressed with hair, feathers, rubber skirts, plastic tails or pork rind. A jig tipped with a plastic crayfish is called a *jig-and-craw*; with

QUICK TIP: Shake a bass jig and then let it rest in place to trigger a strike. Usually a largemouth will inhale the jig after it stops moving.

SECURE A PORK TRAILER, so it can't slide up the shank and foul the hook, by first threading on a grub body.

pork, a *jig-and-pig*. Bass jigs used in heavy cover should have some type of weedguard.

JIGGING SPOONS. These heavy spoons are ideal for jigging vertically in very deep water. Because of their long, thin shape, they resemble a struggling baitfish when jigged erratically.

VIBRATING BLADES. Made of thin metal, these lures produce an intense vibration when jigged vertically. They can also be used like a crankbait.

TAILSPINS. The heavy lead body makes these lures sink rapidly, so they work well for jigging vertically in deep water. The spinner on the tail turns when the lure is pulled up and helicopters when it is dropped back. Tailspins also work well for long-distance casting to schooling bass.

FISHING WEEDLESS SPOONS

Among the oldest of bass baits, weedless spoons are no less effective today than they were a half century ago.

CRAWL A SURFACE SPOON over matted weeds to draw up bass buried beneath the thick vegetation. If you reel too rapidly, the fish won't be able to home in on the bait.

Most weedless spoons have some type of wire, plastic or nylon bristle weedguard to keep the hook from fouling in dense weeds or brush. Some models are intended to run beneath the surface; others to skitter across the surface. Weedless spoons are often tipped with a pork or plastic trailer.

QUICK TIP: Reel a subsurface spoon with a pork-rind attractor through dense vegetation. The lure will have a highly erratic action as it bumps off the weeds.

SUBSURFACE SPOONS. These metal spoons sink rapidly and can be fished through dense vegetation. Because of their heavy body, they can be cast long distances.

Some subsurface spoons have a spinner or propeller at the front end for extra attraction and additional lift.

SURFACE SPOONS. With their light plastic body, these spoons are easy to slide across the surface, so they work well for fishing over matted weeds. But they are not heavy enough for casting to distant targets.

FISHING SOFT PLASTICS

Soft plastics probably account for more largemouth bass than any other type of lure. In fact, plastic worms, which were introduced in the 1950s, soon began catching so many bass that one southern state introduced legislation to ban them! Today, soft plastics are available in three main types.

PLASTIC WORMS. While plastic worms are available in hundreds of shapes and sizes, the majority of largemouth fishermen rely on curlytail plastic worms from 6 to 8 inches in length. These worms are big enough to attract a

QUICK TIP: Custom-color your soft-plastic baits by dipping them in a specially formulated dye, such as Dip-n-Glo®.

good-sized bass, and they have an enticing action when fished at a slow pace. Longer worms, those 10 inches or more, often result in a higher percentage of missed fish. Like other soft plastics, many of the worms manufactured today are scent impregnated for added attraction.

CREATURES. This category includes a wide array of imitation crayfish, lizards, frogs, salamanders, eels, etc. Like plastic worms, these lures come in many shapes and sizes.

SOFT STICKBAITS. These baits have a straight, tapered body designed to swim erratically from side to side with a twitching retrieve. Most soft stickbaits range in size from 4 to 6 inches.

Because largemouth bass are usually found in or around some type of cover, most fishermen prefer to rig their soft plastics Texas-style (opposite page). When rigged Texas-style with a bullet sinker, soft plastics can be fished in the heaviest cover without

QUICK TIP: When fishing a Texas rig or Carolina rig in heavy weeds, use a wooden toothpick to "peg" the sinker. Insert the toothpick in the end of the sinker and break it off flush. Pegging the sinker to the line will help eliminate tangles with weeds.

HOW TO RIG A TEXAS-STYLE WORM

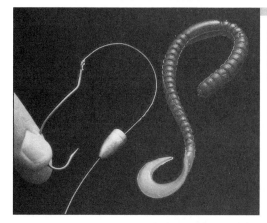

THREAD A BULLET SINKER onto the line, then tie on a worm hook.

INSERT THE HOOK into the worm's head, then thread the first half-inch of the worm onto the hook.

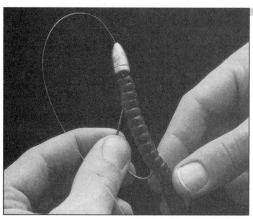

PUSH THE HOOK through, give it a half twist and bury the point in the worm.

HOW TO FISH A TEXAS-STYLE WORM

CRAWL THE WORM along the bottom a few inches at a time, pausing for several seconds between each move. Work it through heavy cover such as weeds, brush or logs. The worm will rarely snag because the hook is concealed.

WATCH YOUR LINE closely at all times. If you see the line twitch slightly or it slowly moves to the side, point the rod tip in the direction of the worm and reel up any slack.

SET THE HOOK immediately with a powerful sweeping motion. Driving the hook through the worm and into the mouth of a bass requires a stiff rod, low-stretch line and a hard hook set.

CAROLINA RIGGING for largemouth bass

hanging up because the hook point is buried in the lure. The disadvantage to this rigging is that during the hook set the hook point must pass through the worm before it penetrates into the mouth of the fish. As a result, your hooking percentage will be lower than if you used an exposed hook.

Another popular rigging method for soft plastics is a Carolina rig (above). This rig differs from a Texas rig in that the bullet sinker is positioned well up the line, rather than riding on the nose of the bait. This way, the bait sinks much more slowly and has a more enticing action. Depending on the density of cover, the hook point may or may not be buried in the bait.

Smallmouth Bass

Wherever there is cool, clear water with a good supply of crayfish, anglers are likely to find smallmouth bass. And, whenever you hook a smallmouth, you're bound to see spectacular leaps and determination unrivaled among freshwater fish.

Prior to 1900, smallmouth bass were found mainly in the Great Lakes and in river systems in the east-central United States. But as the railroads moved west and north, smallmouth were stocked in many rivers, natural lakes and large reservoirs. Probably the most successful introduction was in the clear, rocky lakes of the southern Canadian Shield.

The smallmouth bass is a close cousin of the largemouth, though the species differ in many ways. Smallmouths, for example, prefer slightly cooler water. They are most active in water 67° to 72°F and spawn in water from the upper 50s to lower 60s. While smallmouth spawn in cooler water, they may deposit their eggs a few days later than largemouth. The reason is that shallow, weedy bays used by spawning largemouth warm faster in spring than do the deeper, rocky sites preferred by smallmouth.

Where smallmouth and largemouth inhabit the same waters, smallmouth will usually be found a little deeper and are less likely to inhabit dense, weedy cover.

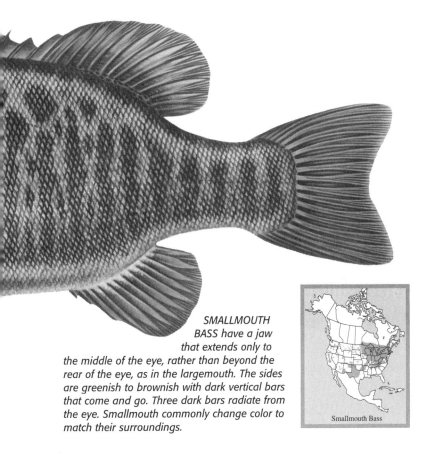

SMALLMOUTH BASS have a jaw that extends only to the middle of the eye, rather than beyond the rear of the eye, as in the largemouth. The sides are greenish to brownish with dark vertical bars that come and go. Three dark bars radiate from the eye. Smallmouth commonly change color to match their surroundings.

Smallmouth Bass

Smallmouth prefer a firm, rocky bottom and, unlike largemouths, are seldom found on soft-bottomed structure.

Smallmouth respond to sunlight and weather changes in much the same way as largemouth. They're most active under low-light conditions and during periods of stable weather.

Although crayfish are the smallmouth's favorite food, they also eat frogs and tadpoles, many kinds of small fish, worms and a variety of insects, including both immature and adult forms.

Smallmouth do not reach the size of largemouth bass. A 5-pound smallmouth is considered a trophy in most waters, though many 7- to 8-pounders are caught each year in Tennessee Valley Authority reservoirs in Kentucky,

Tennessee and Alabama. The world record, caught in Dale Hollow Reservoir, Tennessee, in 1969, weighed 10 pounds, 14 ounces.

Where to Catch Smallmouth in Lakes

Smallmouth bass lakes have one thing in common. They all have at least some rocky bottom to provide spawning habitat for bass. Cool, northern lakes have the largest smallmouth populations, although the biggest fish are caught in deep southern reservoirs such as those created by the Tennessee Valley Authority.

Most of a smallmouth's life is spent in 5 to 15 feet of water. They lurk in the shallows because most of their foods are there and because their eyes are not overly sensitive to bright sunlight. In southern reservoirs, midsummer heat may drive them into 30- to 40-foot depths during midday, though they return to the shallows to feed at dusk.

Smallmouth bass have well-defined territories. Once you find a good spot, you may have to change angling methods with the seasons, but you seldom have to move far to find the fish. Following is a list of prime smallmouth locations in natural and man-make lakes throughout the season.

PRIME LOCATIONS IN NATURAL LAKES

•*Points* attract smallmouth bass throughout the year. Look for long, gradually tapering sand-gravel points with bulrushes, or points made up of golf-ball- to baseball-sized rock.

•*Rocky shorelines* surrounded by deep water are most productive in summer and fall. The best humps taper gradually rather than plunge sharply into the depths.

•*Weedlines* hold smallmouth until the weeds die back in fall. Points and inside turns along the weedline, especially where there is a gravelly or rocky bottom, are key locations.

PRIME LOCATIONS IN MAN-MADE LAKES

•*Rocky shorelines* in protected creek arms draw spawning smallmouth. The best shorelines taper slowly and have scattered boulders that afford protection for the nest.

•*Main-lake points,* especially those that have a rocky bottom and are near the main river channel, are good summertime feeding areas. After feeding, the fish can retreat to deep water.

•*Submerged roadbeds* attract smallmouth because of the hard substrate. Roadbeds are most productive in summer, but shallow ones draw fish in spring and deep ones, in late fall.

Where to Catch Smallmouth in Rivers

Coolwater streams with moderate current and rocky bottoms are favorite smallmouth haunts. Rarely do they live in warm, muddy streams.

River smallmouths prowl rocky shoals to find food. They seldom are found over flat, sandy bottoms. Although they may feed in moderate current, smallmouth spend most of their time in slack water. They commonly lie in current breaks between fast and slow water. Eddies below points, rocks or bridge abutments are favorite hangouts. Often they gather just downstream of trees that have toppled into the water.

Unlike lake-dwelling smallmouth, those in rivers rarely form large schools. Instead, a fish picks out a quiet spot behind rocks or logs, where it lives with one or two other bass. When one is caught, another moves in to take its place. As a result, prime spots always hold bass, despite heavy fishing pressure. Following is a list of these high-percentage spots.

PRIME LOCATIONS IN SMALL RIVERS

•*Boulders* form eddies that make excellent feeding stations for smallmouth in summer and fall. The main eddy forms downstream of the boulder; a smaller one forms just upstream.

•*Bars or points* extending into the river deflect the current and create eddies that hold smallmouth in summer and fall. The fish tend to feed along the current line.

•*Eddies* that form alongside fast water below dams draw smallmouth from late spring into fall. Baitfish that gather in the eddies make easy targets for foraging smallmouth.

PRIME LOCATIONS IN BIG RIVERS

•*Wing dams,* which are man-made current deflectors, draw smallmouth in summer and fall. The fish hold in the eddy just above the wing dam and often feed right on top of the wing dam.

•*Deep cuts* connecting the main channel with backwater areas are most productive in summer and fall. Look for the fish around fallen trees and other objects that break the current.

•*Riprap* is placed along highway or railroad embankments or on islands to prevent erosion. The riprap holds food and provides cover, so it draws smallmouth from spring through fall.

How to Catch Smallmouth

Many smallmouth fishing techniques revolve around the fish's fondness for crayfish. Anglers use rubber-legged jigs, crankbaits and other artificials in brownish or orangish hues resembling the colors of live crayfish. And these lures are usually fished on the rocky bottoms where crayfish live.

But smallmouth also consume plenty of baitfish that are found in weedy or brushy cover or in open water. This explains why spinners, small minnow plugs, twister-tail jigs and other minnow imitations are also considered excellent smallmouth baits.

But smallmouth baits don't have to look like anything in

particular; the fish will hit most anything that makes a lot of commotion. That's why topwater lures, such as stickbaits and propbaits, work so well for smallmouth.

As a rule, smallmouth are aggressive biters, especially where populations are high. It's not unusual to see two or three smallmouth chasing one that's been hooked, trying to steal the lure. The smaller fish are usually the most aggressive.

But there are times when smallmouth are finicky, and that's when live bait outperforms artificials. Besides crayfish, favorite live baits for smallmouth include leeches, nightcrawlers, hellgrammites and minnows, particularly shiners. Fish them the same way you would for walleyes, using slip-sinker or slip-bobber rigs (pp. 136-139). Or, just use a plain hook and a split shot.

Because of the smallmouth's legendary fighting ability, catch-and-release fishing is rapidly gaining in popularity. Without catch-and-release, heavily fished waters could not produce quality smallmouth fishing.

FISHING SUBSURFACE PLUGS

The same types of subsurface plugs used for largemouth work equally well for smallmouth, but smallmouth plugs are generally a little smaller, ranging in length from 2 to 3 inches. When smallmouth are feeding aggressively, however, they will take plugs up to 6 inches long.

QUICK TIP: Wait a few seconds after the plug lands before starting your retrieve. The splash may draw a smallmouth's attention, and it will strike the floating plug.

Crankbaits are a good choice when you want to cover a lot of water in a hurry. The lip tends to deflect off of obstructions like logs and rocks, preventing hang-ups. Be sure to choose a crankbait suitable for the water depth you're fishing. Some models track only a few feet deep; others, more than 20.

Minnow plugs have a realistic look and enticing action that makes them a smallmouth favorite. You can fish them with a steady retrieve or twitch them on the surface. For the most wobble, tie on a minnow plug with a knot that clinches

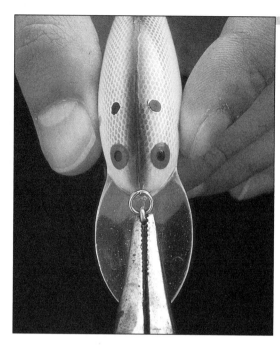

TUNE A SUB-SURFACE PLUG if it is not tracking straight. If the bait is running to the right, bend the attachment eye to the left, and vice versa.

tightly to the attachment eye (such as the Trilene knot, p. 38) and slide the knot toward the bottom of the eye.

Vibrating plugs, when retrieved at high speed, emit a vibration that smallmouth find hard to resist. These lures sink, so you can count them down to any depth. But they are not as snag-resistant as crankbaits.

JIGGING

Jig fishing requires a deft touch, but once you master it, you'll understand why it is considered one of the deadliest smallmouth techniques.

Smallmouth anglers use the same types of jigs and jigging lures used for largemouth, but one of the most effective is a mushroom-head jig tipped with a curlytail grub. Jig heads also work well for presenting live bait. Smallmouth

QUICK TIP: Use two-color jig heads to increase your odds of offering the right color. You can buy them or make your own by dipping heads in fluorescent paint.

will seldom ignore a lively leech, shiner or crawler tipped on a jig head.

Vibrating blades are popular smallmouth baits in man-made lakes throughout the South, but they are a good choice for vertically jigging in any type of water and will easily reach fish at depths of 40 feet or more. Jigging spoons and tailspins can be used for the same purpose.

> QUICK TIP: Cut a piece of pork rind that is too big for small-mouth into smaller pieces about 2 inches long and 1/4 inch wide. Punch a hole in one end of each piece with an awl; the rind may be too tough to penetrate with a hook.

FISHING SOFT PLASTICS

Plastic worms are normally considered a top largemouth bait, but there are times when worms and other soft plastics work just as well for smallmouth. When smallmouth are tucked into dense weeds, for example, a Texas-rigged worm is one of the few baits that will get at them without fouling. Worms used for smallmouth are usually 4 to 6 inches in length, a little shorter than those used for largemouth.

Soft-plastic crayfish and tube baits are good choices for tempting fussy smallmouth. The realistic legs and pincers wiggle enticingly, convincing stubborn fish to strike. These soft plastics should also be a little smaller than the ones used for largemouth.

Although Texas rigs are needed when smallmouth bass are in heavy cover, soft plastics fished on a mushroom-head jig work better when the fish are on a clean bottom, which is most often the case. The open hook will significantly improve your hooking percentage.

TOPWATER FISHING

If you like visual fishing and explosive strikes, try topwater fishing for smallmouth. The technique works best in spring, when smallmouth move into the shallows to spawn. But there are times when topwaters will "call up" smallmouth from water as deep as 20 feet.

Propbaits, stickbaits and chuggers are the most popular

topwaters for smallmouth, but most any high-riding lure will work, including minnow plugs twitched on the surface and spinnerbaits held high enough so the blade almost breaks water.

The best retrieve depends on the mood of the fish. When they're active, a series of twitches with little or no hesitation between them may work best. But when they're finicky, you may have to pause 15 seconds or more between twitches.

Although a topwater strike may be explosive, a smallmouth sometimes just sips in the bait, barely disturbing the surface. Wait until you feel resistance before setting the hook. If you set when you see a splash, you'll probably pull the bait away from the fish.

FISHING SPINNERS AND SPINNERBAITS

A flashing spinner blade appeals to the smallmouth's aggressive nature and predatory instincts. Smallmouth bass fishermen commonly use two different styles of spinners: standard (in-line) spinners and spinnerbaits.

Standard spinners work well in shallow water with little weedy or snaggy cover. Simply cast them out and reel them in just fast enough to make the blade spin. When fishing a bank with a steep, sloping shoreline, cast parallel, rather than perpendicular, to the bank. A parallel cast keeps the lure in productive water longer. A spinner with a

BEND THE SHAFT of an in-line spinner as shown to create a keel effect, which keeps the lure from rotating and putting twists in your line.

size 2 or 3 blade is most effective for smallmouth fishing.

Spinnerbaits are a better choice in weedy or brushy cover because they are resistant to fouling. Most anglers use 1/8- to 1/4-ounce spinnerbaits for smallmouth, but night fishermen often use large spinnerbaits weighing up to 1 ounce. Because cruising smallmouth look up for their food, spinnerbaits should be retrieved fast enough to keep them running no more than a foot beneath the surface. If you don't get a strike within the first 10 feet, quickly reel in and cast again.

QUICK TIP: Start reeling a spinnerbait before it hits the water. Cruising smallmouth are drawn by the frantic action and often strike immediately.

FLY FISHING

Not only is fly fishing one of the most exciting ways to catch smallmouth, it's also one of the most effective. Some flies are nearly perfect imitations of smallmouth foods; others attract smallmouth by the flash or surface commotion they produce. Most smallmouth flies range from size 2 to 6.

Bass bugs, which have bodies made of cork, plastic or clipped deer hair, are fished on the surface, usually with a twitch-and-pause retrieve.

Crayfish flies have lifelike claws made of hair or feathers. Leech flies have a long tail made of marabou or a chamois strip. Many are weighted so they can be fished on the bottom.

Smallmouth anglers also use big streamers that resemble shiners or other minnows, nymphs that look like hellgrammites or immature dragonflies and even dry flies, usually mayfly or stonefly imitations.

Use a fly with a mono weedguard when fishing in snaggy cover. If you tie your own flies, you can easily make a weedguard by tying in a piece of 20-pound mono.

The big, wind-resistant flies used for smallmouth require a weight-forward or bass-bug-taper line, preferably 6-weight to 8-weight.

QUICK TIP: Work a bass bug with your rod tip only a few inches above the water's surface to better control the fly and increase your hooking percentage.

White Bass & Striped Bass

When a school of white bass or striped bass churns the surface in pursuit of baitfish, there is no faster fishing. They instantly strike any lure cast into their midst. And these members of the temperate bass family rank among the strongest-fighting gamefish.

White bass, often called silver bass or sand bass, are found exclusively in freshwater, mainly in big rivers and lakes connected to them, and in large reservoirs. Striped bass, also called rockfish or stripers, are native to the Atlantic coastal waters of North America and, in the late 1800s, were stocked along the Pacific Coast. The fish migrate up major coastal rivers during their spring spawning runs.

When South Carolina's Santee and Cooper rivers were dammed in 1941, striped bass were trapped above the dam. By 1950, stripers were thriving in the newly created reservoir and fishermen were enjoying an exciting new sportfish. The success of stripers in Santee-Cooper led to stocking programs in many other states and to development of the *whiterock* or *wiper,* a white bass/striper hybrid that has been introduced in many southern reservoirs.

White bass and stripers have similar lifestyles. Both

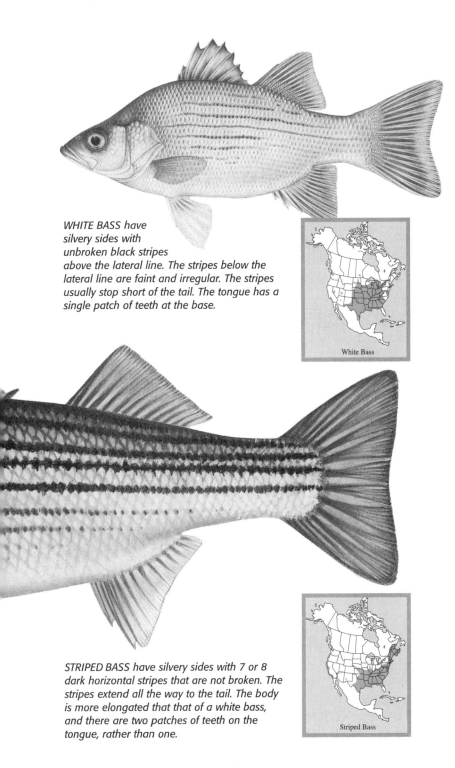

WHITE BASS have
silvery sides with
unbroken black stripes
above the lateral line. The stripes below the
lateral line are faint and irregular. The stripes
usually stop short of the tail. The tongue has a
single patch of teeth at the base.

White Bass

STRIPED BASS have silvery sides with 7 or 8
dark horizontal stripes that are not broken. The
stripes extend all the way to the tail. The body
is more elongated that that of a white bass,
and there are two patches of teeth on the
tongue, rather than one.

Striped Bass

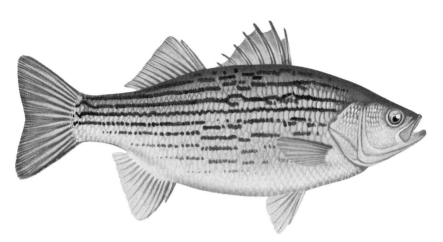

HYBRIDS have silvery sides with dark stripes that are broken both above and below the lateral line. The body depth is intermediate between that of the white bass and striped bass. Hybrids are infertile; they do not occur in nature and must be stocked.

species migrate up rivers and streams in spring, spawning when the water temperature reaches about 58°F. Similarly, they both prefer large bodies of water that have an abundance of gizzard or threadfin shad, their primary food. They are rarely linked to structure or cover; instead, they roam wide expanses of open water following schools of baitfish.

The pack-feeding behavior of white bass and stripers makes them an easy target for anglers. When foraging bass tear into a school of shad, the baitfish flip out of the water in an attempt to escape, often drawing flocks of sea gulls. Savvy fishermen look for the gulls diving into the water, quickly motor to the edge of the melee and then cast into the swirling water.

White bass rarely exceed 3 pounds, while stripers often weigh more than 30. The record white bass, caught in Lake Orange, Virginia, in 1989, weighed 6 pounds, 13 ounces. The largest striper taken from inland waters, 67 pounds, 8 ounces, was caught in O'Neill Forebay, California, in 1992. The record hybrid, 25 pounds, 15 ounces, came from Warrior River, Alabama, in 1996.

Where to Catch White Bass and Stripers

White bass and stripers are constantly on the move. A school of hungry bass may appear out of nowhere, providing fantastic fishing for several minutes, and then disappear just as quickly.

Huge schools of white bass and stripers migrate upstream in spring, stopping in pools and eddies along the way. They move upriver until a dam, waterfall or other obstruction blocks their progress.

After spawning, both species retreat downstream where they scatter into the open water of lakes or reservoirs. They spend most of the summer in water from 20 to 40 feet deep. At daybreak and dusk, they move onto shallow sand flats to chase schools of shad or shiners.

By late summer or fall, young-of-the-year shad have grown large enough to interest the bass, and the pack-feeding behavior mentioned earlier begins. White bass and stripers may slash into a school of shad at any time of day.

In the North, late fall and winter fishing is slow because feeding diminishes greatly in water cooler than 50°F. But ice fishing for white bass can be outstanding if you can locate the spots where large schools winter. In the South, fishing for both white bass and stripers remains good through the winter months. In winter, the fish spend less time roaming open water and are more likely to tuck into heavy cover, such as flooded timber. Following is a list of the top locations for finding and catching white bass and stripers throughout the year.

PRIME WHITE BASS AND STRIPER LOCATIONS

•*Dams* stop the spring spawning migration of white bass and stripers. The fish congregate in eddies or slack water near the fast current, where they feed on shad, shiners and other small baitfish.

•*Back ends of creek arms* attract spawning white bass and stripers in reservoirs. The fish are drawn into the back ends

91

by warm water and flow from inlet streams.

•*Edges of sand flats* are excellent white bass and striper spots in summer and fall. The fish rest in the deep water and move up on the flat to chase shad and other baitfish early and late in the day.

•*Main-lake points,* especially those with extended, sandy lips, concentrate white bass and stripers in summer and fall. Often, the fish move onto the points to feed in early morning.

•*Warmwater discharges* from power plants attract huge schools of shad during winter. The shad, in turn, draw white bass and stripers, offering fast fishing for anglers willing to brave the elements.

•*Deep water* along the dam face holds shad, stripers and white bass during the winter months. The zone just above the dam usually has the reservoir's deepest, warmest water.

How to Catch White Bass and Stripers

The techniques for catching white and striped bass are similar, but stripers demand tougher equipment and bigger baits. For white bass, use a light- to medium-power spinning outfit with 4- to 8-pound-test line; for stripers, a medium-heavy- to heavy-power spinning or baitcasting outfit with 15- to 40-pound-test.

Both species are easiest to catch during the spring spawning period. When thousands of fish are concentrated in the tailwaters of a dam or the back end of a creek arm, they strike most any bait tossed their way.

Once the fish complete spawning and scatter into open water, finding and catching them becomes a lot tougher. That's when trolling techniques work best, because they enable anglers to cover wide expanses of water. Once a school is located, some fishermen stop and jig spoons or lead-head jigs straight below the boat.

In waters with good populations of threadfin or gizzard shad, fishing picks up again in fall as the fish begin tearing into large shad schools on the surface. Then, anglers switch to a technique called jump-fishing (below).

In the North, white bass are sometimes taken by ice fishing. The fish congregate in huge, very tight schools, and if you can locate one, you can expect some fast action.

JUMP-FISHING

When you spot a flock of gulls circling and diving into the water, there's a good chance that they've located a school of white bass or stripers tearing into a mass of shad. During the onslaught, many of the shad are injured, providing the bass with an easy meal.

Should you see such a feeding frenzy, get to the spot in a hurry. But don't motor right up to the school with your outboard or you'll spook the school. Instead, stop well

USE AN ELECTRIC MOTOR to edge within casting distance of the school. If you run your outboard, the vibrations may spook the fish.

CHOOSE JUMP-FISHING LURES about the size of the baitfish that white bass and stripers are eating.

short of the school and quickly move up to the school using your electric trolling motor. If you're careful not to get too close to the fish and spook them, the action may last for an hour or more. If you're not, they'll be gone within seconds and you'll have to look for another school.

Some fishermen rig one rod with a topwater and another with a jig or diving plug. Then, if one presentation fails to produce, they can quickly switch to the other rig and avoid wasting time.

White bass anglers often rig two or more jigs on the same line. When a bass grabs one jig, other bass give chase in an attempt to steal it. They spot the other jig and you haul in a pair of fish.

TROLLING

The trolling methods used for white bass are simple; just toss a small crankbait, vibrating plug or jig behind the boat and troll through an area that is known to produce white bass.

But trolling for stripers gets a lot more complicated. Anglers use downriggers and side planers to spread their lines vertically and horizontally, maximizing their coverage. In spring and fall, when the water is cool, most trolling is done in the upper 25 feet. In summer, however, you may have to get your lines into 40 to 60 feet of water. That's when downriggers are a must.

Threadfin Shad

Gizzard Shad

CHOOSE GIZZARD SHAD instead of threadfin shad whenever possible. Gizzard shad work better for bait because they are hardier and grow to a larger size. You can distinguish between the two by differences in coloration. The gizzard shad has a blackish margin on the tail; the threadfin, yellowish. To keep shad lively while trolling, push the hook through the shad's nostrils (right). Use a 2- to 3-ounce egg sinker about 4 feet above the hook to get the shad down deep.

Most striper fishermen troll very slowly, using a bow-mount electric motor to avoid spooking the fish. If you can find a source of live shad or net your own, they make excellent bait. Hook shad through the nostrils with a size 2/0 hook. If shad are not available, use a bucktail or horsehead jig tipped with a curlytail grub.

Once you locate a school of white bass and stripers, switch to a technique that gives you more thorough coverage, like jigging. Continue to work the spot until the school disperses, then resume trolling.

Originally developed in the 60's as a saltwater lure, the

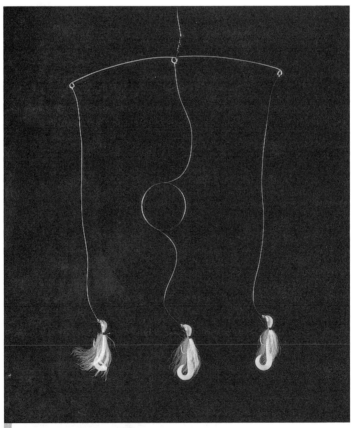

MAKE A SPREADER RIG by bending a piece of stiff wire as shown. A spreader enables you to troll three jigs at a time on a single line and keeps them tracking far enough apart so they don't tangle.

umbrella rig, or spreader rig (opposite page), creates the illusion of a school of bait and can account for great catches.

TOPWATER FISHING

The commotion made by a topwater lure appeals to the aggressive feeding instincts of white bass and stripers. Topwaters work best around spawning time, when the hungry predators are chasing baitfish in the shallows. But they can be effective anytime the fish are feeding in shallow water, particularly early and late in the day.

Small stickbaits and propbaits, from 2 to 3 inches long, are the best choice for white bass. Fish a stickbait with a walking-the-dog retrieve; a propbait, with a brisk, steady retrieve.

Stripers find it hard to resist large, noisy popping plugs. Some of these plugs are nearly a foot long. When you see a fish swirl on the surface, cast the plug several feet past the swirl, then retrieve it with a series of powerful jerks for maximum splash.

Floating minnow plugs worked on the surface also account for good numbers of stripers. Just cast the lure out and retrieve it slowly enough that it makes a noticeable wake.

OTHER WHITE BASS AND STRIPER TECHNIQUES

The aggressive nature of white bass and stripers means that they're vulnerable to a wide variety of presentations.

Casting with lead-head jigs has long been a popular method. The fish seem to prefer jigs fished with a straight retrieve rather than an erratic jigging action, but often it pays to mix up your retrieves to see what works best on a given day.

Vertically jigging with lead-heads or jigging spoons is a favorite deep-water method, but it also works well for jump-fishing (p. 93). While one angler casts to the surface feeders, another vertically jigs for fish that remain on the bottom.

Balloon fishing with live shad is one of the most effective methods for trophy stripers. A balloon tied to the line

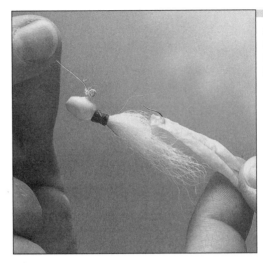

ATTACH A ¼-inch by 1¼-inch-long strip of belly meat to the jig.

with an overhand knot will keep a large shad afloat, yet the shad can easily tow the balloon around, covering all the water around your boat. When a striper bites, line slips through the balloon, causing it to bob erratically.

Striper fishermen also troll or drift using a live or cut shad or herring on a tandem-hook harness. White bass anglers sometimes tip their jigs with strips of white-bass belly meat (above) when fishing gets tough.

Fly fishing for white bass and stripers is gaining in popularity. Any bright-colored streamer will catch white bass. For stripers, try bulky streamer patterns tied with materials that "breathe" in the water.

Sunfish

The near-universal popularity of sunfish is easy to understand. For a youngster just learning to fish, they are one of the easiest fish to catch. For an expert, catching big sunfish is as much of a challenge as catching big bass or pike. For an angler interested in sport, sunfish put up a great fight on light tackle. And for those who enjoy eating fish, their sweet-tasting meat is unsurpassed as table fare.

The sunfish family includes crappies, black bass and true sunfish (genus *Lepomis*). When anglers use the term "sunfish," they are referring to the latter. The largest and most important to fishermen are the bluegill, redear and pumpkinseed. In the South, sunfish are often collectively referred to as *bream* (pronounced "brim"). Many types of true sunfish do not grow large enough to interest anglers.

Hybridization is common among sunfish species. Practically every kind of sunfish will crossbreed with every other kind that inhabits the same waters. The result is numerous varieties of sunfish that even experts have trouble identifying.

Sunfish begin to spawn in spring, at water temperatures from the upper 60s to low 70s. They have a strong homing instinct and return to spawn in the same vicinity each year. The male builds a nest on a sand or gravel bottom, at depths from 6 inches to 3 feet. The nests, which are round, light-colored depressions, are often very close together, forming a spawning colony.

After depositing her eggs, which may number more than 200,000, the female abandons the nest. The male stays on to guard the eggs and, later, the fry. The male is very aggressive and will attack anything that comes near the nest, including a fisherman's bait.

Sunfish may spawn several times over the course of the summer. Multiple spawning attempts are more common in the South than in the North. In the South, the fish commonly spawn around the full moon.

Sunfish have a varied diet consisting mainly of

larval and adult insects, crustaceans, mollusks and, sometimes, small fish. They rely heavily on sight and scent to find their food. Although they usually feed in the morning and early evening, they may also feed during midday. Sunfish bite in sunny or cloudy weather. Night fishing is best on clear nights with a bright moon or around lighted docks.

Despite heavy fishing pressure, sunfish often overpopulate a body of water because they produce too many young. This results in high competition for food and a low growth rate. Under these conditions, none of the fish attain large size. The biggest sunfish are caught in southern waters and, throughout the North, in lakes and ponds with relatively low sunfish populations.

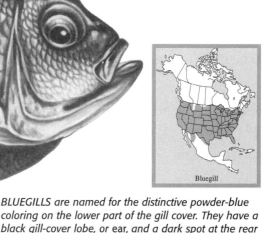

Bluegill

BLUEGILLS are named for the distinctive powder-blue coloring on the lower part of the gill cover. They have a black gill-cover lobe, or ear, and a dark spot at the rear base of the dorsal fin. The world record, 4 pounds, 12 ounces, was caught in Ketona Lake, Alabama, in 1950.

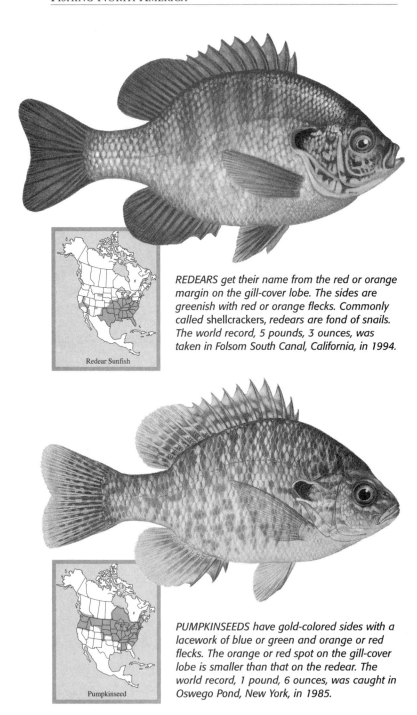

Redear Sunfish

REDEARS get their name from the red or orange margin on the gill-cover lobe. The sides are greenish with red or orange flecks. Commonly called shellcrackers, redears are fond of snails. The world record, 5 pounds, 3 ounces, was taken in Folsom South Canal, California, in 1994.

Pumpkinseed

PUMPKINSEEDS have gold-colored sides with a lacework of blue or green and orange or red flecks. The orange or red spot on the gill-cover lobe is smaller than that on the redear. The world record, 1 pound, 6 ounces, was caught in Oswego Pond, New York, in 1985.

Where to Catch Sunfish

Sunfish can survive in most any kind of warmwater environment, including ponds, strip pits, natural lakes, man-made lakes and rivers of any size. The fish are rarely found in coldwater lakes or streams, except in shallow weedy bays or backwaters where the water is much warmer.

Many anglers prefer to fish for sunfish around spawning time, when they're heavily concentrated and aggressively feeding. As a rule, the fish bite best at water temperatures above 60°F, but you can catch them any time of the year. Some north-country fishermen would argue that sunfish bite best just after freeze-up.

Sunfish do most of their feeding in daylight hours. Peak fishing times are early and late in the day, but you can catch some fish all day long. Weather is not much of a factor in fishing for sunfish, although a strong cold front may slow the action.

Following are some of the best places to find sunfish in their most important habitats.

PRIME LOCATIONS IN NATURAL LAKES

• *Shallow, weedy bays* with sand-gravel shorelines make good spawning areas. Sunfish return to these areas in fall and stay through early winter.

• *Points with stands of bulrushes* or other emergent vegetation are sometimes used for spawning and may hold sunfish into early summer.

• *Extended lips of points,* especially those with plenty of submerged vegetation, are good sunfish producers from late spring into fall.

• *Weedy humps* are prime summertime sunfish locations. The bigger fish usually hold along the deep edge of the weedline.

PRIME LOCATIONS IN MAN-MADE LAKES

• *Back ends of creek arms* warm earliest in spring and draw sunfish in to spawn. The best creek arms are fed by clear water creeks.

A FAVORITE TIME for anglers is the spawning time, when sunfish are heavily concentrated and aggressively feeding.

•*Creek channel edges* are excellent summertime locations. The fish find cover among the flooded timber and can easily retreat to deep water in the channel.

•*Main-lake points* that slope gradually into deep water hold sunfish in summer and fall. Sunfish often suspend in open water just off the points.

•*Deep holes* at the lower end of creek arms hold large numbers of sunfish in winter. The holes serve as staging areas for fish that will swim up the arms to spawn in spring.

PRIME LOCATIONS IN RIVERS

•*Brush piles* offer cover and give sunfish a spot where they can get out of the current. New brush piles with plenty of small twigs are best.

•*Weedy backwaters* of medium- to large-size rivers hold sunfish year-round. They offer food, cover and a place to escape the current.

•*Eddies* that form below obstructions such as points, boulders and log jams provide the slack-water habitat that river-dwelling sunfish require.

HOW TO CATCH SUNFISH

Bobber fishing with live bait, such as worms, small leeches, grasshoppers, crickets, grass shrimp and waxworms, accounts for more sunfish than any other method. However, tiny jigs and other small artificials fished with ultralight tackle can be equally effective. And when sunfish are concentrated in the shallows, particularly at spawning time, fly fishing with poppers or wet flies may be the best technique of all.

QUICK TIP: Use a long-shank hook when fishing with live bait. Sunfish often take the bait deeply, and the long shank makes hook removal much easier.

When fishing with a bobber rig (below), use 2- to 6-pound mono with a size 8 long-shank hook. About 10 inches from the hook, add enough split shot so the bobber barely floats. Normally, the bait should be 6 to 18 inches off the bottom. Alternately jiggle the bobber and then let it rest. Most bites come after the bait stops moving.

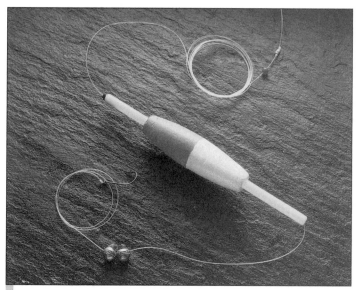

TYPICAL BOBBER RIG for sunfish with 2- to 6-pound mono and a size 8 long-shank hook.

Good electronics are a big help in sunfish fishing. You can easily spot large schools adjacent to cover or suspended in open water. Then, all you have to do is put your bait at the right depth and you'll have instant action.

QUICK TIP: *Place your bait in hard-to-reach spots, such as pockets in the weeds, using a 10- to 14-foot extension pole or cane pole. Lift the fish out vertically.*

FLY FISHING

If you like fast action, try casting a popper onto a sunfish spawning bed on a warm spring evening.

Bluegills are the most surface-oriented of the sunfish. Besides poppers, they will also slurp in sponge bugs, dry flies and terrestrials. Redears, or shellcrackers, which feed mainly on snails, are less likely than bluegills to take surface offerings.

Most any small wet fly or nymph fished near the bottom will catch all types of sunfish.

USE A POPPER with a nymph dropper to catch sunfish in shallow water. The popper will attract the aggressive fish and the nymph will catch the neutral fish.

Crappie

The popularity of crappie fishing has skyrocketed in recent years. Outdoor magazines are now devoting more space to the sport, and there are even crappie-fishing tournaments with huge purses.

Crappies can be one of the easiest fish to catch, but they are one of the hardest to find consistently. Their nomadic habits mean that they seldom stay in one place for more than a few days at a time. They are quite predictable around spawning time, however, explaining why most anglers focus on that period.

Although crappies begin congregating in shallow bays shortly after ice-out, they are moving in to feed on baitfish drawn by the warm water, not to spawn, as many anglers believe. Spawning does not begin until the water reaches about 64°F. Males make a nest by fanning away debris on a sand, gravel or rock bottom, often among emergent vegetation such as bulrushes. Females scatter soon after spawning, but males stay around to guard the nest until the fry are old enough to leave.

One reason crappies are so hard to pattern is that they often feed on plankton suspended in open water, straining it through their closely spaced gill rakers. They also eat small fish, larval aquatic insects and a variety of crustaceans.

Crappie populations are cyclical. The fish can be extremely abundant for a few years, but then the population begins to thin out and fishing becomes difficult. No one knows for sure why this happens.

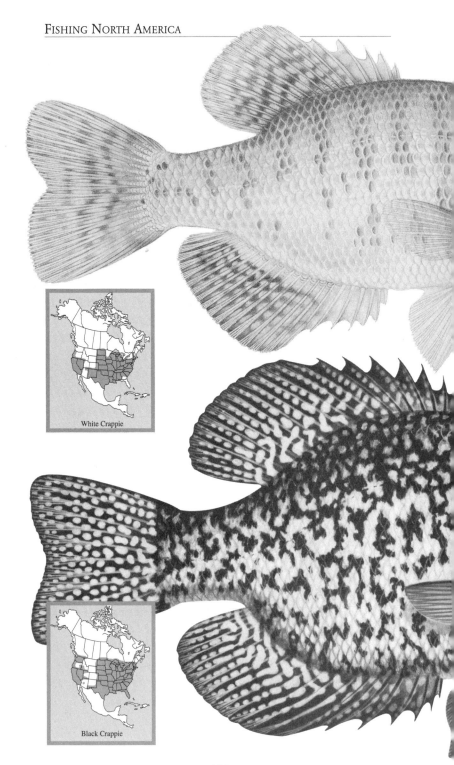

White Crappie

Black Crappie

There are two species of crappies: black and white. Black crappies are more abundant in the North; white crappies prevail in the South. However, their ranges overlap considerably. White crappies are often found in turbid lakes; black crappies require clearer water.

Crappies are one of the prettiest fish in fresh water. Anglers have given them more than 50 colorful names including calico bass, specks, strawberry bass, papermouths and bachelor perch.

WHITE CRAPPIES have dark speckles set in vertical bars. Dorsal spines number 5 or 6. The body is more elongated than that of a black crappie and the forehead has a sharper depression. World record: 5 pounds, 3 ounces; Enid Dam, Mississippi, 1957.

BLACK CRAPPIES have irregular dark speckles across the sides. The dorsal fin has 7 or more spines. The world-record black crappie, 4 pounds, 8 ounces, was caught in Kerr Lake, Virginia, in 1981.

Where to Catch Crappies

Crappies are found in nearly every state and in many waters of southern Canada. They live in most warmwater lakes and in the slow-moving stretches of warmwater rivers. Black crappies favor hard bottoms with plenty of weedy cover. White crappies are found on hard or soft bottoms with lots of woody cover, particularly sunken brush. In waters where cover is scarce, both black and white crappies often use man-made fish attractors such as sunken coniferous trees.

Although crappies are usually found near some type of structure or cover, they sometimes roam open water in search of food. Finding them can be difficult because they may suspend over the deepest part of a lake.

Crappies feed both day and night, although the prime feeding time is usually around dusk. In clear lakes, they often bite best at night. Crappies can be caught any time of the year, but feeding slows considerably at water temperatures below 50°F.

Like bluegills, crappies tend to overpopulate many waters, causing the fish to become stunted. Anglers seeking big crappies should fish waters where the population is relatively low. Following are some of the best spots to find crappies in natural lakes, man-made lakes and rivers.

PRIME LOCATIONS IN NATURAL LAKES

•*Shallow bays* with dark bottoms warm much earlier in spring than the main lake, drawing baitfish, which, in turn, draw hungry crappies.

•*Emergent vegetation,* particularly bulrushes, makes ideal spawning cover for crappies. Look for the old, brown bulrushes, not the new-growth green ones.

•*Rock piles* and weedy sunken islands with deep water nearby are good summertime locations. Crappies can find baitfish around the rocky or weedy cover.

•*Deep holes* hold crappies in late fall and winter. Most of the weeds in shallower water have died off, and the deep water is a few degrees warmer.

PRIME LOCATIONS IN MAN-MADE LAKES

•*Entrances to creek arms* hold crappies in late winter and early spring, before spawning time. Look for the fish near the creek channel or off deep points.

•*Back ends of creek arms* with plenty of brushy cover draw spawning crappies. Some fish also spawn on brushy points in creek arms.

•*Edges of creek channels* or the main river channel attract crappies in summer. The fish usually hold in the flooded timber.

•*Deep stretches* of the main river channel or deep creek

channels concentrate crappies in late fall and winter. Deep points also draw fish.

PRIME RIVER LOCATIONS

•*Brushy sloughs* are important spawning locations. Look for the spawning crappies along sand-gravel, rather than mud, banks.

•*Deep backwaters* hold crappies most of the year. The best backwaters have plenty of cover, such as weeds, stumps, fallen trees or brush piles.

•*Eddies* in the main river channel give crappies a place to escape the current. Large eddies below points and dams are prime crappie locations.

How to Catch Crappies

Crappie anglers rely heavily on minnows or lures that resemble them. Minnows are usually fished on a slip-bobber rig set to keep the bait slightly above the depth

HOOK MINNOWS according to angling technique. For bobber fishing, hook the minnow behind the dorsal fin (top). When trolling, hook it through the lips (middle). For jigging, hook the minnow in the head or through the eye sockets (bottom).

THE COUNTDOWN METHOD FOR SUSPENDED CRAPPIES

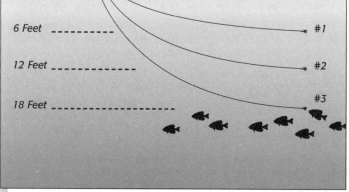

6 Feet .... #1

12 Feet .... #2

18 Feet .... #3

CAST A JIG, then count as it sinks. With 6-pound line, a ½-ounce jig drops about 1 foot in 1 second; a ⅛-ounce jig, about 2 feet.

Begin your retrieve at different counts until you find crappies. With a ⅛-ounce jig, retrieve #1 (started at 3 seconds) and retrieve #2 (6 seconds) pass too far above the fish. But retrieve #3 (9 seconds) draws a strike. If you know where fish are located, count down to 1 to 2 feet above that depth.

of the fish. Most anglers hook minnows behind the dorsal fin for bobber fishing and through the lips, head or eye sockets for casting or trolling.

Lure choice depends on the depth of the crappies. Jigs and small, deep-diving crankbaits are best in water deeper than 10 feet. In shallower water, try small spinners or spinnerbaits, minnow plugs or spoons.

A slow, erratic retrieve is normally best, although crappies occasionally strike fast-moving lures. Twitching the lure, then allowing it to settle back, may entice stubborn crappies to bite. They usually grab the lure as it sinks. The countdown method (above) works well for casting jigs or other sinking lures to suspended crappies.

Light tackle with 2- to 6-pound-test line is adequate for most crappie fishing. When fishing in stumps or brush piles, however, you'll need 10- to 17-pound line to avoid constant break-offs. When using a float, make sure you balance it with enough weight so the fish feel little resistance when they take the bait.

QUICK TIP: Set a slip-bobber so your bait rides just above the weeds. Let the bobber drift. A strong wind will lift the bait too far above the weeds, so you must add more weight or lower the bait by readjusting the bobber stop.

When crappies are in the shallows, fly fishing with bright-colored wet flies and small streamers ranks among the most effective techniques. Crappies seldom feed on the surface, so poppers are not a good choice.

The crappie nickname *papermouth* comes from the paper-thin membrane around the mouth. Once you hook a crappie, do not set the hook again or try to horse the fish in, because the hook may tear out of its mouth.

FLY FISHING

Wet flies and small streamers rank among the deadliest of all crappie lures, especially in spring, when spawners move into the shallows.

If you can see spawning crappies in the shallows, cast to the darker-colored fish, which are the males. They're considerably more aggressive than the females.

Once crappies leave the shallows, they can be difficult to find, and fly fishing is not nearly as effective.

Yellow Perch

Yellow perch rank among the tastiest of freshwater fish, so it's not surprising that they're so popular. Closely related to walleyes and saugers, perch live in many of the same waters, but they are rarely abundant where water clarity is very low. The largest populations are in clear, northern lakes with moderate weed growth. Perch have been stocked in many southern waters.

Like walleyes and sauger, perch are coolwater fish, preferring water temperatures from the mid-60s to low 70s. But they feed throughout the year and, in the North, are a favorite of ice fishermen.

Yellow perch spawn soon after the ice goes out in spring, usually when the water reaches about 45°F. They lay their eggs in jellylike bands that cling to rocks, plants and debris on the bottom. Staggering numbers of young are hatched, much to the benefit of predators such as largemouth bass, northern pike and walleyes.

Important perch foods include immature aquatic insects, crayfish, snails, small fish and fish eggs. Adult perch do most of their feeding on or near the bottom and are not as likely to suspend as sunfish or crappies. Because of their poor night vision, perch feed only during the day.

In many waters, perch become too abundant and, as a

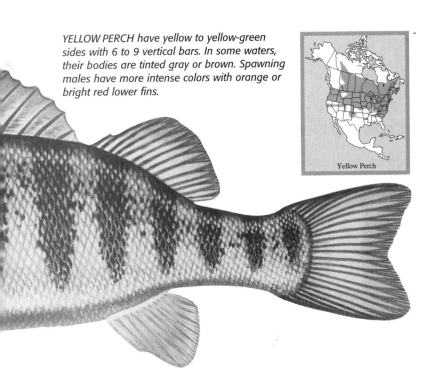

YELLOW PERCH have yellow to yellow-green sides with 6 to 9 vertical bars. In some waters, their bodies are tinted gray or brown. Spawning males have more intense colors with orange or bright red lower fins.

Yellow Perch

result, never reach a size large enough to interest fishermen. A 7- to 8-inch perch is acceptable to most anglers, but perch often grow much larger. The world record, 4 pounds, 3 ounces, was caught in the Delaware River, New Jersey, in 1865.

How to Catch Yellow Perch

The gluttonous feeding habits of yellow perch make them an easy target for anglers. You can catch them any time of year; in fact, some of the most impressive catches are made by ice fishermen.

Live bait fished near the bottom accounts for the majority of yellow perch. You can fish the bait on a plain size 4 to

6 hook, usually with a slip-sinker or split-shot rig, or use it to tip a lead-head jig or a jigging spoon.

Perch are found in many of the same spots that hold walleyes (p. 132). Look for them in shallow bays and on shallow flats in early spring and on points, weedy or rocky humps and irregular breaklines the rest of the year.

Most yellow-perch anglers rely on light spinning tackle with 4- to 6-pound mono. The fish are not strong fighters, and the light tackle helps cast the small baits and lures.

USE A THIN STRIP of belly meat from a perch or a minnow head instead of a whole minnow when perch are striking short. The belly meat or minnow head provides necessary scent and your hooking percentage will be much higher.

Catfish

Although catfish do not get a lot of press, they rank near the top of the popular gamefish list. Only bass and panfish have a larger following. If you have ever battled a very large cat or dined on fresh catfish fillets, you can easily understand why these bewhiskered fish have so many fans.

Flathead and blue catfish commonly exceed 50 pounds and many topping 100 pounds have been taken, but most were not officially documented. Channel catfish weighing more than 20 pounds are scarce, though some big rivers produce much larger ones. White catfish, the smallest kind, rarely exceed 5 pounds.

Channels and flatheads are the most common catfish species. Blue catfish populations have declined in many areas, but huge blues are still caught in parts of the central and southern United States. White catfish are confined mainly to the East and West Coasts.

Catfish thrive in medium- to large-size warmwater rivers, or in lakes connected to rivers. Most warmwater impoundments have good catfish populations. Catfish can tolerate extremely muddy water and even moderately high levels of pollution. Unlike bullheads, they can't live in waters prone to winterkill.

The highly varied diet of catfish consists mainly of fish, fish eggs, insect larvae, mollusks, crustaceans and aquatic

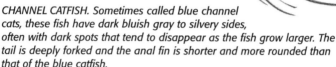

CHANNEL CATFISH. *Sometimes called blue channel cats, these fish have dark bluish gray to silvery sides, often with dark spots that tend to disappear as the fish grow larger. The tail is deeply forked and the anal fin is shorter and more rounded than that of the blue catfish.*

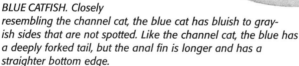

BLUE CATFISH. *Closely resembling the channel cat, the blue cat has bluish to grayish sides that are not spotted. Like the channel cat, the blue has a deeply forked tail, but the anal fin is longer and has a straighter bottom edge.*

plants. They also eat dead and rotting organic material.

All species of catfish have an acute sense of smell, and their whiskers, or *barbels*, are equipped with taste buds. They can easily find food in muddy water or after dark by probing the bottom with their barbels as they swim along. Their well-developed senses of smell and taste explain the effectiveness of *stinkbaits*.

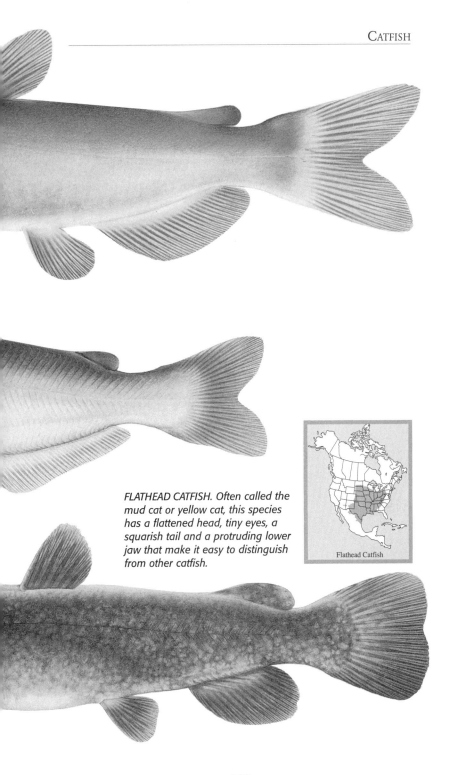

FLATHEAD CATFISH. Often called the mud cat or yellow cat, this species has a flattened head, tiny eyes, a squarish tail and a protruding lower jaw that make it easy to distinguish from other catfish.

Flathead Catfish

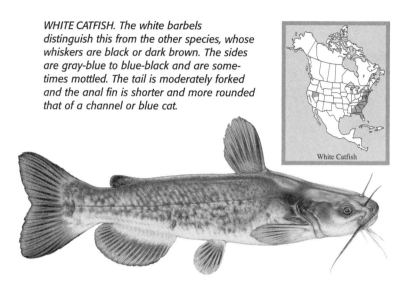

WHITE CATFISH. The white barbels distinguish this from the other species, whose whiskers are black or dark brown. The sides are gray-blue to blue-black and are sometimes mottled. The tail is moderately forked and the anal fin is shorter and more rounded that of a channel or blue cat.

White Catfish

Catfish start to spawn in late spring when the water temperature reaches about 70°F. They have a curious habit of spawning in enclosed areas such as sunken barrels, hollow logs, muskrat runs and other holes in riverbanks.

Following are world records for each of the catfish species:

Channel – 58 pounds, Santee-Cooper Reservoir, South Carolina, 1964.

Flathead – 123 pounds, 9 ounces; Elk City Reservoir, Kansas, 1998.

Blue – 111 pounds, Wheeler Reservoir, Alabama, 1996.

White – 18 pounds, 14 ounces; Withlacoochee River, Florida, 1991.

Where to Find Catfish

Catfish have an affinity for woody cover. You'll find them on brushy flats, in flooded timber and around "snags" – trees or parts of trees that wash into river pools.

In small rivers, finding catfish is not much of a problem. You simply look for the deep holes, especially the ones with plenty of snags. In big rivers and reservoirs, however, catfish are harder to find because they move a lot more. Like most other gamefish, they follow the forage. They also move to find comfortable water temperatures.

In late fall, for instance, cats migrate great distances to reach warmwater discharges of power plants. In the warmer water, they feed all winter.

Big-river cats also migrate to reach deep wintering holes. Often, thousands of fish can be found in a hole of only a few acres. These wintering catfish are dormant and seldom bite; divers have been known to grab them and carry them to the surface.

Water stage plays a major role in catfish movement. When the water is low, they tend to move into deep holes and stay put. When it's rising, they are drawn into shallow creek arms and backwaters.

Catfish avoid sluggish or stagnant water. They sometimes feed in fast current, but more often, you'll find them in the slower water alongside it. Blue cats prefer faster water than channels or flatheads, often holding in swift chutes or pools with moderate current.

Catfish bite best at night, but can be caught during the day, especially after a heavy rain when river levels are rising. Then, even midday fishing can be good. Catfishing slacks off when the water temperature drops below 55°F. At temperatures below 40°F, they rarely feed.

Following is a list of some of the best spots to catch catfish in rivers and reservoirs.

PRIME RIVER LOCATIONS

•*Running sloughs* have an inlet and outlet connecting them to the main channel, so they always have noticeable current. They draw catfish in summer and fall.

•*Riprap shorelines* brushed by a light current make good feeding areas for catfish in summer.

•*Wintering areas* are deep holes, often near the mouth of a tributary. Huge schools of catfish traditionally congregate in the same holes each winter.

•*Outside bends* in small to medium-size rivers are natural holding areas for catfish most of the year; the strong current along a bend usually excavates a deep hole.

•*Deep pools* in small rivers may provide the only suitable resting areas for catfish. Often, the fish do their feeding in the riffle just upstream of the pool.

•*Tailwaters* below dams draw catfish because of the abundant supply of forage fish. Most of the cats hold in the deepest washout holes.

PRIME RESERVOIR LOCATIONS

•*Brushy creek arm*s are important catfish spawning areas. These areas also draw catfish under rising water conditions.

•*Wooded flats,* especially those near spawning sites, serve as feeding areas for catfish in summer and fall.

•*Wooded points* offer a combination of structure and cover that is attractive to catfish throughout the year.

•*Old creek channels* and flooded stock tanks provide the deepwater retreat that catfish require in late fall and winter.

How to Catch Catfish

Although you may occasionally catch a catfish on a jig, spinner, crankbait or other artificial lure, the vast majority of cats are taken on natural or prepared baits. And there are times when cats take baits suspended from a float, but bottom rigs account for by far the most of them.

The list of catfish baits is nearly endless. You can catch cats on soap, congealed chicken blood, entrails of small animals, freshwater clams that have rotted in the sun for a day or two, dead birds, mice, frogs, worms, crayfish, grasshoppers, Limburger cheese, doughballs and any number of homemade or commercially produced stinkbaits. Live or dead fish, especially those with high oil content such as gizzard shad and smelt, are effective because they give off a scent that carries a long distance.

Any kind of catfish may grab any one of these baits, but flatheads are most likely to take live baitfish; channels, dead or prepared baits. Blues and whites are intermediate in their bait preferences.

Equipment for catfish angling need not be sophisticated,

but it should be heavy-duty. For fishing around snags and rocks, you'll need 20- to 50-pound-test line. This way, you can turn a big catfish before it can wrap your line around an obstruction and break free. In the strong current of a tailrace, you may need up to a pound of weight to keep the bait on bottom and prevent it from drifting.

SLIP-SINKER FISHING

Slip-sinker fishing is the simplest and most popular catfishing method. All you have to do is toss out your bait, prop your rod up on a forked stick or place it in a rod holder and wait for a bite. When the fish swims off with your bait, the line flows freely through the sinker, so the fish won't feel resistance and let go.

Baits that emit scent are ideal for slip-sinker fishing. Currents carry the scent to the catfish and they follow the scent trail to the bait. So if you're in a good catfish spot and have enough patience, the fish will eventually come to you.

When a catfish does take your bait, wait for it to stop running, rapidly wind in slack until you feel the fish's weight, then set the hook as hard as you can. Keep enough pressure on the catfish so it cannot take the line into a snag.

If you're fishing for huge catfish, you can probably get by without a slip-sinker. A big cat won't drop the bait just because it feels a little resistance. That explains why many veteran catfish anglers weight their line with just about any heavy object they can find, including old bolts, spark plugs and other discarded hardware items.

CHUMMING

In the world of catfishing, chumming is relatively new, but anglers throughout the South are finding it to be a highly reliable method.

Most often, chumming is done with fermented grain, such as wheat, milo or cracked corn. The chum mixture (p. 124) is prepared several days ahead of time to allow for sufficient fermentation.

The chum should be spread in early morning, at least one hour before you plan on fishing and, preferably, a little sooner. Be sure to chum every spot that you will fish during the day.

There are two main reasons why chumming improves catfishing success. Scent from the chum spreads quickly, attracting catfish from a large area and concentrating them in a much smaller area. And the chum starts what amounts to a "feeding frenzy," so the fish are feeding more actively than they otherwise would. So when you drop your bait into the middle of a foraging school, you often get a bite within seconds.

> CHUM RECIPE: Fill three 5-gallon buckets two-thirds full of wheat, milo or cracked corn. Add 1 cup of sugar to each bucket. Add water until the level is a few inches above the grain. Cover the buckets and allow 2 days for the grain to absorb the water. Then, refill the buckets so the water level is again a few inches above the grain; reseal. Allow the grain to ferment 5 days at a temperature of 75°F; 3 days at 90°.

Chumming is especially effective for channel catfish; flatheads and blues are less likely to respond to rotting or fermented baits. Chumming works well any time of year, any time of day and under any weather conditions.

DRIFT-FISHING

Drift-fishing does not rank among the most popular catfishing methods, but when blues and flatheads are scattered over large flats, as is often the case in summer, it is one of the most effective.

Up to a half dozen 8- to 9-foot-long rods are placed in rod holders set along the gunwales on both sides of the boat. The lines are rigged with a 1- to 2-ounce sinker and a chunk of cut bait, such as mullet or shad, on a size 4/0 to 6/0 wide-bend hook. Be sure to set the lines so they fish just inches off bottom and adjust them periodically as the depth changes.

As the boat drifts over a likely catfish flat, the lines cover a swath of water more than 20 feet wide. When you finish your drift, motor upwind and make another drift to cover a different swath. Keep changing drift paths until you locate the fish.

Small catfish may peck at the bait, but a big one will pull the rod tip down and keep it down. When you see a rod tip bend over, set the hook immediately.

JUG FISHING

Most anglers think of catfish as bottom feeders, but there are times when cats suspend in midwater to feed on sunfish and other baitfish.

Free-floating jugs are often rigged with a 50-pound monofilament dropper line that has 4 to 6 size 2/0 hooks equally spaced to cover the entire depth spectrum (below). A 2- to 3-ounce sinker holds the dropper line in a vertical position. The line should almost, but not quite, reach bottom.

Jug fishing is simple. Just put your favorite bait on the hooks and then release the jugs upwind of the area you want to fish. Or let them drift down a river. You can let your boat drift with the jugs or let them drift on their own, coming back to check them later. When you see a jug dancing, pick it up and pull in your cat.

A TYPICAL jug-fishing rig

125

Bullhead

All you need is an old lawn chair, a cane pole and a can of angleworms to fill a gunnysack with bull-heads.

Prime time for bullhead fishing is late spring and summer, after the water temperature has reached at least 60°F. Bullheads may feed anytime during the day, but become more active toward evening when they cruise the shallows for insect larvae, snails, worms, fish eggs and small fish. Bullheads also eat a variety of aquatic plants. Like catfish, bullheads rely on an acute sense of smell, plus taste buds in their barbels, to find food. This explains why they bite so well after dark.

Bullhead fishermen generally use two or three small worms on a long-shank hook. The long hook provides additional leverage for removing the barb from a bullhead's mouth. Because bull-heads have poor eyesight, the exposed shank

BLACK BULLHEADS have greenish to gold sides that are not mottled. The barbels are grayish to black. The tail has a slight notch and there is usually a pale bar at the base. The anal fin is rounded and the pectoral spines are weakly barbed. The world-record black bullhead, 8 pounds, was caught in Lake Waccabuc, New York, in 1951.

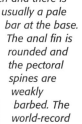

Black Bullhead

BROWN BULLHEADS have yellowish to brownish sides, usually with distinct mottling. The barbels are dark brown to black. The tail, which is square or slightly notched, does not have a pale bar at the base. The anal fin is rounded and the pectoral spines are strongly barbed. The world record, 6 pounds, 1 ounce, was taken in Waterford, New York, in 1998.

Brown Bullhead

YELLOW BULLHEADS have yellow to yellow-brown sides with no mottling. The chin barbels are whitish to pinkish; the upper barbels, brown. The anal fin has a straight lower edge and the tail is rounded. The world-record yellow bullhead weighed 4 pounds, 4 ounces. It was caught in Mormon Lake, Arizona, in 1984.

Yellow Bullhead

does not keep them from biting. Most anglers attach a small rubber-core sinker and fish the worms on the bottom. Some add a bobber and dangle the bait just off the bottom.

Slow-moving rivers, shallow lakes or ponds are favorite bullhead spots. Black bullheads tolerate the muddiest water; browns and yellows prefer clearer water with more weeds.

Because bullheads are so resilient, populations often become stunted from overcrowding. In freeze-out lakes, bullheads often outlast other fish species, because they require only minute amounts of oxygen. Bullheads have been known to survive in lakes that freeze almost to the bottom by simply burrowing several inches into the soft ooze.

Bullheads are delicious if caught in spring and early summer, but as the water warms, their flesh softens and may develop a muddy taste. Fishermen should be extremely careful when handling or cleaning bullheads, because their pectoral spines are coated with a weak venom and can inflict a painful wound. Always grab a bullhead as shown below to avoid the sharp dorsal and pectoral spines.

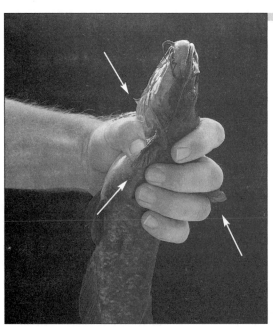

HOLD A BULL-HEAD as shown to avoid the sharp dorsal and pectoral spines (arrows).

Walleye & Sauger

Walleye and sauger are creatures of darkness. Like deer, owls and many other animals that are active at night, they have a layer of pigment, called the *tapetum lucidum,* in the retina of the eye. This light-sensitive layer enables them to see well even in murky or dimly lit water, a fact important to fishermen. The sauger has a larger tapetum than the walleye, making its eyes even more light sensitive.

Walleye and sauger may inhabit the same waters, though sauger are primarily a river species. When found in the same waters, saugers usually go deeper than walleyes, because of their light-sensitive eyes.

The two species are quite similar in appearance, but they can be easily distinguished by the white tip on the lower part of the walleye's tail and the rows of black spots on the sauger's dorsal fin. Walleye and sauger sometimes hybridize to produce *saugeyes.*

Classified as coolwater fish, walleye and sauger are usually found in water from 60° to 70°F in summer. Spawning begins in spring when the water warms to the mid- to upper 40s, which means early March in the South to mid-May in northern climates. Sauger spawn about a week later than walleye. Fishing is good just before spawning but is very difficult once spawning begins. The action picks up again about 10 days after spawning has been completed.

Although some walleyes survive longer than 20 years, most live 10 years or less. In the South, walleyes may reach 2 pounds in only 3 to 4 years and fishermen annually catch 15- to 20-pounders. In northern waters, where growth is slower, it takes about 6 years for a walleye to reach 2 pounds and an 8-pound fish is considered a trophy.

Saugers are shorter-lived, rarely surviving past 13 years. Southern saugers grow to a weight of 2 pounds in about 4 years; in the North, it may take 7 years to reach that size. But northern saugers are longer lived and reach a larger size.

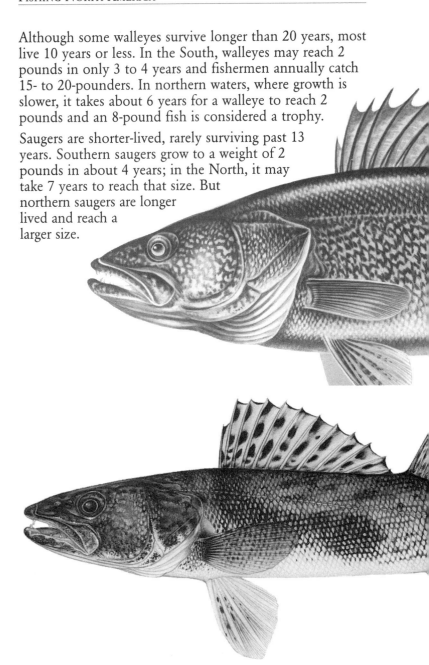

WALLEYE. The sides are olive-green with gold flecks and the belly varies from white to yellow-gold. The spiny (front) dorsal fin is not spotted, but has a black blotch at the rear. There is a white tip on the lower lobe of the tail. World record: 22 pounds, 11 ounces; Greer's Ferry, Arkansas, 1982.

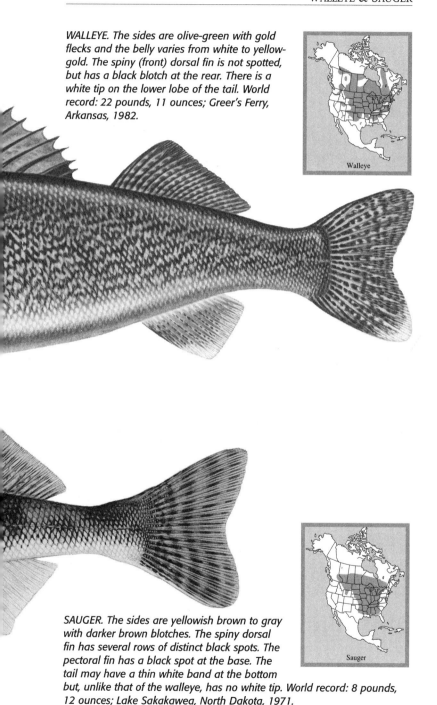

Walleye

SAUGER. The sides are yellowish brown to gray with darker brown blotches. The spiny dorsal fin has several rows of distinct black spots. The pectoral fin has a black spot at the base. The tail may have a thin white band at the bottom but, unlike that of the walleye, has no white tip. World record: 8 pounds, 12 ounces; Lake Sakakawea, North Dakota, 1971.

Sauger

Where to Find Walleyes and Saugers

Walleyes and saugers are highly mobile. Tagging studies have shown that they may swim more than 100 miles to reach a desired spawning area. They also move vertically in response to changes in light penetration, water temperature and oxygen content.

In spring, the fish remain in warm shallows for several weeks after spawning, usually in water no more than 20 feet deep. They can stay in the shallows all day, because the low angle of the sun's rays has little effect on their light-sensitive eyes.

As summer approaches, the shallows become too warm and the sun rises higher in the sky, forcing the fish to retreat to cooler depths. However, they may move shallower to feed in morning and evening. Walleyes rarely go deeper than 30 feet, but saugers may go as deep as 50.

In fall, the fish move shallower as the surface begins to cool. Once again, the sun is low on the horizon, so the fish can feed in shallow water all day. But the fall turnover scatters the fish and may push them deeper. By the time the surface temperature drops into the 40s, they may be as deep as 50 feet.

Oxygen content also affects walleye and sauger location. In summer, many fertile lakes lack oxygen in the depths, so the fish are forced to remain in the shallows, sometimes in depths of 10 feet or less.

Following is a list of some of the best spots in natural lakes, man-made lakes and big rivers to catch walleye and sauger.

PRIME LOCATIONS IN NATURAL LAKES

•*Bulrush beds* on shallow points and reefs draw walleyes and saugers in spring and late fall. Fish hold along the edges.

•*Gravel-rubble shorelines*, especially those exposed to the wind, make excellent spawning habitat.

•*Gradually sloping points* close to the spawning grounds attract post-spawn walleyes and saugers.

•*Deep reefs and humps,* particularly those connected to other structure by a saddle, are good midsummer spots.

•*Sharp-dropping points* in the main lake produce walleyes and saugers from late summer to late fall.

•*Irregular breaklines* hold more walleyes and saugers in summer and fall than a breakline with few points or inside turns.

PRIME LOCATIONS IN MAN-MADE LAKES

•*Rocky main-lake points* are prime locations in summer. Points with an extended lip where the fish can feed are better than points that drop off rapidly.

•*Deep pools* in tributary streams concentrate pre-spawn walleyes and saugers and often produce some of the year's biggest fish.

•*Sharp-sloping points* near the old river channel draw fish in fall. After feeding on the points, the fish can move to deep water in the river channel to rest.

•*Riprapped embankments* make good spawning habitat and will often hold fish into early summer.

PRIME LOCATIONS IN BIG RIVERS

•*Tailwaters* of major dams hold walleyes and saugers from late fall through spawning time in early spring. The fish concentrate in eddies alongside the fast current.

•*Wing dams* make ideal feeding areas from late spring through fall. Walleyes often feed right on top of the wing dam; saugers, in deeper water off the front or back slope.

•*Rocky shorelines* with light current attract walleyes and saugers in summer and fall. Rocky bottoms produce more food than sandy or muddy bottoms.

How to Catch Walleye and Sauger

Walleyes and saugers are known for their finicky feeding habits. Although there are times when they will slam most any artificial lure you throw at them, they normally have to be teased and tempted, often with some type of live bait. In fact, live-bait presentations account for the majority of walleyes and saugers taken.

The techniques for catching walleyes and saugers are nearly identical, the difference being that saugers are normally caught in deeper water.

Live bait can be fished on a slip-sinker or slip-bobber rig, pulled behind a spinner, tipped on a jig or simply fished with a plain hook and split shot. But whatever technique you choose, location is of the utmost importance.

Walleyes and saugers are schooling fish, often clustering tightly on small structural elements, like points, inside turns and patches of rocky bottom. Consequently, your presentation must be precise in order to keep your bait in the strike zone.

This explains why boat control is such an important part of walleye and sauger fishing. You must be able to work a spot very slowly while keeping your bait at a consistent depth. Such control normally requires an electric trolling motor.

But the fish are not always linked to exact spots. They sometimes scatter over large flats or even suspend in open water. At these times, you need to cover more water, so the most productive methods are trolling with plugs or spinner rigs.

Side planers and downriggers, used mainly in trout and salmon fishing, are gaining popularity among walleye enthusiasts. These devices enable you to cover more water than you otherwise would, and to precisely control your fishing depth.

Electronics play a huge role in walleye fishing. Without a good graph, for instance, you'd find those tight schools of fish only by accident. On big water, it would be nearly impossible to return to a productive spot without a GPS unit.

SPINNER FISHING

Trolling with a spinner and live bait is one of the oldest walleye techniques, and it is just as effective today as ever. Spinners work equally well for saugers, but are used less frequently.

Most fishermen rely on spinner rigs with size 2 to 4 blades. In clear water, silver, gold or brass blades usually work best. In murky water, choose fluorescent orange or chartreuse. A rig with a single size 4 to 6 hook works best for minnows or leeches; a double- or triple-hook rig is a better choice for crawlers, because it will catch the short strikers.

Spinner rigs must be weighted to get them to the bottom. You can add a sinker to the line a few feet ahead of the rig, but many anglers prefer to use a 3-way-swivel or bottom-bouncer rig to keep the spinner off the bottom. A 1/2-ounce sinker will get you down to a depth of about 10 feet. Add about 1/2 ounce more weight for each additional 5 feet.

A different type of spinner, called a weight-forward spinner, is very popular on the Great Lakes. Fishermen usually put a nightcrawler on the spinner so that no more than an

USE A LONG-SHANK HOOK to catch short strikers when fishing a spinner and minnow. Insert the point of the hook though the mouth and out the gill, and then push the hook through the back.

inch of the worm trails behind the hook. To locate walleyes with a weight-forward spinner, you simply cast it out, count it down to different depths, and retrieve it fast enough to keep the blade turning.

SLIP-SINKER FISHING

Walleyes and saugers are notorious for picking up the bait and then dropping it as soon as they feel resistance. A slip-sinker rig eliminates this resistance, allowing the fish to swim away on a free line after grabbing the bait.

All you need to tie a basic slip-sinker rig are a hook, sinker and stop. When you pull the rig ahead, the stop catches the sinker and moves it along. But when a fish bites, it pulls the line the opposite way and the sinker stays put.

The sinker is probably the most important component. It must be heavy enough to get the rig to the bottom. As a rule, you'll need 1/8 ounce of weight for every 10 feet of depth. Most anglers use an egg sinker or walking sinker, but a bullet sinker works better in weedy cover.

The length of the leader must also be considered. When walleyes and saugers are near bottom, there is no need for a long leader. An 18- to 36-inch leader works well in this situation. But when the fish are suspended, you may need a leader over 10 feet long.

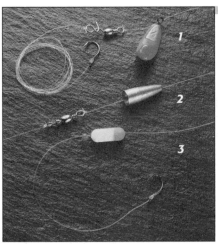

SLIP-SINKER RIGS are available with (1) walking sinkers, for clean or rock bottom, or (2) bullet sinkers, for weedy bottom. Rigs with a (3) float ahead of the hook lift your bait above a blanket of weeds or reach fish that are holding a little off the bottom.

HOW TO FISH A SLIP-SINKER RIG

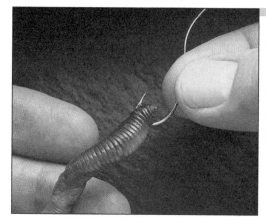

HOOK A MINNOW through the lips; a leech, just above the sucker and a nightcrawler, through the tip of the head and out the side, about 1/4 inch from the tip.

HOLD THE LINE with your index finger as you troll or drift; keep the bail open.

RELEASE THE LINE when you feel the slightest tug. Let line flow freely off the spool until the fish stops running. Then point the rod at the fish and quickly reel up slack until you feel some resistance. Then set the hook with a sharp snap of the wrist.

SLIP-BOBBER FISHING

When walleye or sauger fishing gets tough, you can often tempt the fish to bite by dangling the bait right in their face. The best way to do this is to suspend it from a slip-bobber rig. This type of rig is also effective when walleyes and saugers are suspended at a certain depth, or when they are holding on a small piece of structure like an isolated rock pile.

A slip-bobber works better than a fixed bobber for fishing in deep water. With a fixed bobber set at more than a few feet, you would not be able to cast the rig.

HOW TO FISH A SLIP-BOBBER RIG

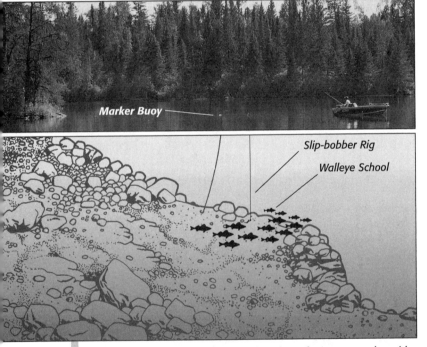

DROP A MARKER BUOY on a promising piece of structure or alongside a school of walleyes that you spotted on your graph. Position your boat within casting distance of your marker, then toss out a slip-bobber rig set to the right depth. Even negative fish have a hard time ignoring a bait dangled right in their face.

You can make a slip-bobber rig by knotting a piece of string or rubber band on the line at the desired fishing depth. Thread on a small bead and then the bobber. Add split shot for balance. Tie on a size 4 to 6 hook and bait with a leech, crawler or minnow. For night fishing, use a lighted float powered by a tiny lithium battery.

JIG FISHING

A jig is the ideal lure for walleyes and saugers. It sinks quickly into the depths they inhabit and it is designed to be worked slowly to tempt fussy biters. Most walleye and sauger fishermen tip their jigs with live bait for extra attraction, regardless of whether the jig already has a soft plastic, feather or hair dressing.

How you work a jig depends on the mood of the fish. When the water is cold and the fish sluggish, a very slow, gentle jigging action usually works best. But when the water warms and the fish become more aggressive, try a more intense jigging action.

The usual way to work a jig is to cast it out, let it sink to the bottom, then retrieve it with a series of twitches and pauses. After each twitch, you must keep the line taut while the jig sinks back to the bottom. The fish usually strike when the jig is sinking, and if your line is not taut, you won't feel a thing. Sometimes you'll feel a distinct tap

TIP A JIG with a minnow by (1) pushing the hook through the lips, from the bottom up. To keep a minnow on the jig longer, (2) hook it through the eye sockets. The most secure method of attaching a minnow is to (3) insert the hook point into the mouth and then push it out the top of the head. Hook a leech (4) through the sucker end.

when a fish strikes; other times, the jig may just stop sinking prematurely or you may just feel a little extra resistance. Whenever you feel anything different, set the hook.

A sensitive, fast-action rod is a must for jig fishing. It helps you feel even the lightest tap and gives you an immediate hook set, so the fish can't spit the jig before you respond.

TROLLING WITH PLUGS

Trolling has long been an effective way to catch walleyes and saugers, but with the advent of walleye tournament fishing, the popularity of this technique has skyrocketed. Trolling is the best way to locate fish in unfamiliar waters, because it enables you to cover a lot of water in a hurry.

In years past, trolling simply meant tossing out a lure behind a moving boat. But modern trollers use a variety of devices, such as side planers and downriggers, that greatly increase their efficiency. Side planers spread your lines horizontally, while downriggers precisely position them vertically.

REEL IN A FEW TURNS when you feel the plug bumping bottom; let out more line if you haven't felt it bump for a while. Continue to adjust your depth as you troll along. When a fish strikes, it usually hooks itself.

VARY THE ACTION and speed of the plug by periodically sweeping the rod tip forward, then dropping it back. The change often triggers a strike from a fish that has been following the plug.

Deeper-running plugs have also improved the troller's success. Some crankbaits now dive to a depth of 30 feet with no added weight. Experienced trollers know which plugs to select when they want to fish a particular depth.

Low-stretch, thin-diameter braided lines have been a big help, as well. These lines have less water resistance, so plugs run deeper than with ordinary lines. And because they don't stretch, you'll get much better hook sets.

Northern Pike & Muskie

These top-rung predators are the subject of great disagreement among fishermen. Some regard big pike and muskies as the ultimate gamefish – powerful fighters that will test even the most skilled angler. Others consider them voracious killers that decimate populations of more desirable gamefish.

With their long, powerful body, huge head and razor-sharp teeth, it's easy to understand why these fish have such a fearsome reputation. It is not uncommon for a pike or muskie to strike a bass or walleye struggling on a fisherman's line.

In North America, three members of the pike family are of interest to fishermen. They include the northern pike, muskellunge and chain pickerel. Grass and redfin pickerel are caught occasionally, but they rarely exceed 12 inches in length.

Lakes with shallow, weedy bays or connecting marshes have the highest pike populations, but the fish can adapt to most any kind of water. Muskies are less adaptable; they require clearer water and a higher oxygen content.

Pike spawn soon after ice-out, beginning when the water reaches about 40°F. They scatter their eggs onto dense vegetation in shallow bays or marshes. Muskies spawn several

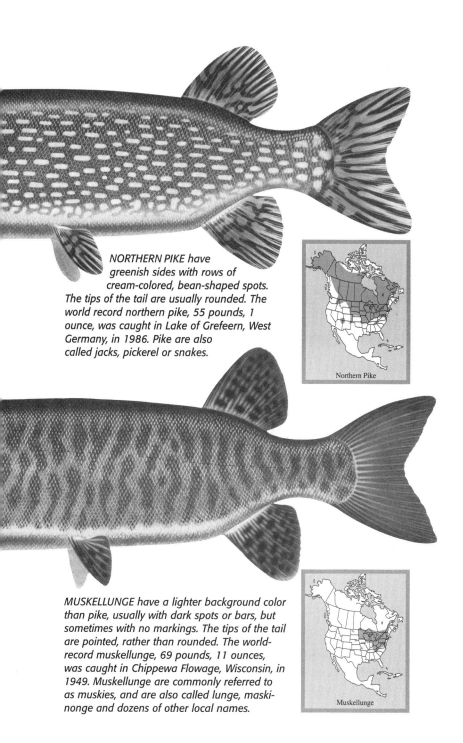

NORTHERN PIKE have greenish sides with rows of cream-colored, bean-shaped spots. The tips of the tail are usually rounded. The world record northern pike, 55 pounds, 1 ounce, was caught in Lake of Grefeern, West Germany, in 1986. Pike are also called jacks, pickerel or snakes.

Northern Pike

MUSKELLUNGE have a lighter background color than pike, usually with dark spots or bars, but sometimes with no markings. The tips of the tail are pointed, rather than rounded. The world-record muskellunge, 69 pounds, 11 ounces, was caught in Chippewa Flowage, Wisconsin, in 1949. Muskellunge are commonly referred to as muskies, and are also called lunge, maski-nonge and dozens of other local names.

Muskellunge

weeks later, at a water temperature of 49° to 59°F in slightly deeper water.

Pike and muskies are opportunists, feeding on whatever prey they can find. They may eat muskrats, mice, turtles, salamanders, small ducks and other birds, but most of their food is fish, preferably cylindrical-bodied fish that slide down easily. They commonly take fish one-half their own body length.

Willing biters, pike often follow a lure, hitting it repeatedly until hooked. Because pike are so easily caught, the large ones can be readily skimmed off a population. Today, most pike weighing over 20 pounds are taken in remote northern lakes and rivers where fishing pressure is light. Muskies are much harder to catch, commonly following a lure all the way to the boat and then turning away at the last second. This explains why muskies often reach 35 pounds or more, even in heavily fished waters.

Where and When to Find Pike and Muskies

Locating small northern pike is not much of a challenge. They spend nearly all of their time in shallow, weedy water from 2 to 15 feet deep. But finding big pike is not as simple. They are found along with the small ones in spring, but when the shallows warm in summer, they scatter into 20- to 40-foot depths where they can be hard to locate. Good-sized muskies also spend more time in deep water than do small ones, but the tendency is not as strong as it is in pike.

Summertime pike fishing is difficult if the water gets too warm. If pike cannot find water cooler than 75°F, they feed very little. Pike feed actively through the winter months, however, and are a frequent target of ice fishermen.

Muskies prefer warmer water than pike and are seldom found in waters that don't reach at least 68°F in summer. This explains why their range does not extend as far north. Muskies are much less active than pike in winter and are rarely caught by ice anglers.

Pike bite best during daylight hours; the action begins to slow at sunset and night fishing is seldom worthwhile. Fishing is usually better on overcast days than on sunny ones. Muskies are much more likely to feed at night.

Anglers in clear lakes have discovered that night fishing with big, noisy surface lures is a deadly muskie technique. Like northerns, muskies seem to bite best under cloudy skies.

Tagging studies have shown that pike are highly mobile, going wherever they must to find food. Muskies move about much less, so when you spot a big one, remember the location and fish it again at a later date. Following is a list of prime northern pike and muskie locations in natural lakes, man-made lakes and rivers.

PRIME LOCATIONS IN NATURAL LAKES

•*Weedy bays* make good spawning areas. Pike prefer to spawn in shallower bays than do muskies.

•*Weedy humps,* especially those covered with cabbage, hold pike and muskies in summer.

•*Weedy saddles* connecting two pieces of structure, like a point and an island, are good spots in summer.

•*Narrows* usually have currents that attract baitfish. They hold pike and muskies in summer and fall.

•*Rock reefs* near deep water produce pike and muskies from summer through early fall.

•*Stream mouths* draw baitfish, which, in turn, attract pike and muskies through the open-water season.

PRIME LOCATIONS IN MAN-MADE LAKES

•*Shallow coves* in creek arms warm early in spring and attract spawning pike and muskies.

•*Timber-covered humps* in the main lake, especially those near the main river channel, hold fish in fall.

•*Points* projecting into creek channels hold pike and muskies that have just finished spawning.

PRIME RIVER LOCATIONS

•*Backwater lakes* make good spawning areas in big rivers.
The fish may stay in deep backwaters all year.

•*Weedbeds* are excellent pike and muskie producers from
late spring until the weeds turn brown in fall.

•*Deep pools* with light current are good year-round pike and
muskie locations in smaller rivers.

How to Catch Northern Pike and Muskie

Whether you prefer live bait or artificial lures, one basic
rule applies in pike and muskie fishing: use big bait if you
want to catch big fish. A good guideline is to select a bait
about one-fourth the length of the fish you expect to
catch. Go a little smaller in early spring or under cold-
front conditions.

Many pike and muskie anglers make the mistake of using
tackle that is too light. When they finally get the strike
they've been waiting for, they fail to hook the fish because
their rod was too flimsy to drive the hooks into the fish's
bony mouth. Or, they hook the fish and then lose it
because of a broken line.

A medium-heavy power baitcasting outfit spooled with 12-
to 25-pound monofilament or braided line is ideal for most
northern pike fishing. For muskies, use a heavy power baitcasting rod with 30- to 50-pound line.

Whatever outfit you choose, be sure to attach a wire leader.
The fishes' sharp teeth will easily shear off monofilament
or braided line.

Because muskies (and sometime pike) have the irritating
habit of following a bait to the boat and then turning
away at the last instant, fishermen should learn the figure-
eight maneuver. Reel the lure to within about a foot of the
rod tip and, with the tip well beneath the surface, begin
making large figure-eight patterns. Often the quick change
of direction will entice the fish to strike.

Most experienced anglers release big pike and muskies to fight again. But some fisherman make the mistake of bringing these fish into the boat where they may thrash around uncontrollably and injure themselves. If possible, use a longnose pliers and carefully unhook them in the water.

FISHING BUCKTAILS AND SPINNERBAITS

Pike and muskies find it hard to resist the vibration and flash of a big spinner blade. Large in-line spinners are usually called *bucktails,* because of the deer-hair tail dressing. But the dressing may also consist of feathers or some kind of synthetic material. Spinnerbaits are more weedless, because of their upturned single hook and safety-pin shaft.

Bucktails and spinnerbaits are normally fished by casting, especially when you're working specific targets, such as a dense clump of weeds or a downed tree. But they can also be trolled to cover large flats or weedlines.

In spring, try a spinner from 3 to 5 inches long. Later,

ATTACH A Snap-Loc® bell sinker of the appropriate weight to the split-ring or wire loop that holds the treble hook. These sinkers make changing or removing weight easy.

TIP A SPINNER-BAIT with a live minnow or a plastic grub for extra attraction. Don't use minnows or grubs more than 4 inches long or you'll get too many short strikes.

when the water warms, try a 6- to 10-incher. You can regulate the depth at which the bait tracks by changing your retrieve speed and rod angle. When you want the bait to run deeper, slow down your retrieve and keep your rod tip low. For even more depth, let it sink for a few seconds before you start reeling. To keep the bait shallow, reel faster and hold your rod tip high. With a little practice, you can make the blades "bulge" the surface, creating a wake that attracts fish.

FISHING TOPWATERS

Not only is topwater fishing one of the most exciting ways to catch pike and muskies, there are times when it is one of the most effective.

When the fish are buried in dense weeds, for example, most other lures would foul in the vegetation. But the noise and surface disturbance from a topwater will draw the fish out of the weeds.

Topwaters work best from late spring through early fall, when water temperatures are warmest. They are much less effective in cold water.

Fishermen use a variety of topwaters for northern pike and muskies. Buzzbaits have a double- or triple-winged blade on a straight or safety-pin shaft. Stickbaits are long, slender plugs with no built-in action; they dart from side to side when you give the rod a series of sharp downward twitches. Propbaits have a propeller at one or both ends. Crawlers have a cupped face or arms that produce a wide wobble and a gurgling sound.

FISHING SUBSURFACE PLUGS

It's no wonder that subsurface plugs work so well for pike and muskies – their wobble and vibration mimic that produced by a swimming baitfish, the primary pike-muskie food.

The trick to fishing with subsurface plugs is to select one that runs at the depth you want to fish. If you're casting to a weedbed that tops off at 3 feet, for instance, it makes no sense to use a bait that runs at 10 feet; you'll spend all your time picking weeds off the hooks. Conversely, if the fish are holding at the base of a deep weedline, a shallow runner would not get down far enough to draw a strike.

There are four basic types of subsurface plugs. Crankbaits have a broad front lip, which gives them a strong wobble. Minnow plugs have a narrower lip and slimmer body, so their wobble is less intense but more natural. Trolling plugs have an extra-wide wobble, because of their broad, flattened head. Vibrating plugs have no lip and the attachment eye is on the flattened back, giving them a very fast, tight wiggle.

JERKBAIT FISHING

As their name suggests, jerkbaits are designed to be fished with a series of jerks of the rod, which imparts an erratic darting action much like that of an injured baitfish.

The majority of jerkbaits are floaters, although many anglers add weight to the hooks or body of the lure to get it down a little deeper.

Jerkbaits are normally fished with a series of sharp, downward twitches of the rod to achieve a side-to-side or up-and-down action. Jerkbait fishermen normally use short, stiff rods so the rod tip does not hit the water on the downward stroke.

Jerkbaits vary widely in shape, size and action, but most of them fall into two categories: gliders, which dart from side to side, and divers, which dart downward. Divers generally run deepest and, because they have little lateral movement, will track through sparse weeds better than a lure with broad side-to-side movement.

FISHING SPOONS

These traditional pike-muskie baits are no less effective today than they were decades ago. One reason spoons work so well is that they're versatile. In most cases, you troll or retrieve them at a steady pace, but you can also use an erratic stop-and-go retrieve, jig them vertically in deep water or skitter them across the surface.

The main decision you must make when selecting spoons is thickness of the metal. Choose a thick spoon for distance casting; a thin one for maximum wobble.

If you'll be fishing in dense weeds or other heavy cover, select a weedless spoon. Add a pork strip or soft-plastic curlytail for extra attraction. Most of these baits have only a single hook; to improve your hooking percentage, make sure it is needle-sharp.

When fishing with spoons, attach them to a flexible, braided-wire leader. This way, they will have an enticing wobble. A thick wire leader restricts their action too much.

JIGGING

Most anglers do not associate jigs with pike and muskie fishing. Yet there are times when jigs will outproduce all other artificials.

A slow-moving jig is hard to beat in early spring or late fall, when cool water temperatures make the fish lethargic and unwilling to chase lures like bucktails and topwaters. Jigs are also effective after a cold front or when fishing very clear water.

The most important considerations in jig selection are weight and head shape. If your jig is too light, you'll have a hard time keeping it close to the bottom, especially in a strong wind. Pike and muskies often strike a jig as it's sinking. If the jig is too heavy, it will sink faster than it should, giving the fish less time to make the decision to strike. Jigs for pike-muskie fishing normally weigh 3/8 to 7/8 ounce.

An ordinary roundhead jig is adequate for fishing on a clean bottom, but in weedy cover you'll need a brushguard jig. A swimmer head will keep the jig riding above the weeds. In late fall, when muskies are found on deep rock piles, pyramid jigs dragged along the bottom are most effective.

FLY FISHING

A big pike or muskie can test the skill of even the most accomplished fly fishermen. Luckily, the fish tend to make relatively short runs, so if you take your time and don't try to horse them in, you'll be able to tire them out and land them.

Pike and muskies are most vulnerable to fly fishing in spring. Warming water draws them into shallow weedy bays where they are easily taken on divers, poppers, sliders and large streamers. When the fish go deep in summer, you'll need weighted flies and sinking lines to reach them.

Depending on the size fish you expect to catch, select flies ranging from size 2 to 4/0. If you'll be fishing in weeds, brush or logs, be sure your fly has a mono or wire weedguard.

You'll need a 7- to 10-weight rod and a weight-forward line to cast these heavy, wind-resistant flies. Most anglers use a 6- to 9-foot leader with an 8- to 14-pound-test tippet and a 12- to 30-pound shock tippet made of multi-strand coated wire.

LIVE-BAIT FISHING

Only a few decades ago, live baitfish accounted for about three-fourths of all pike and muskies caught by anglers. That percentage is considerably lower today, but there are times when the fish are interested in nothing but baitfish.

When the bite is off because of cold water or for any other reason, baitfish will still produce. The majority of anglers use live baitfish, primarily suckers, chubs and shiners from 5 inches to more than a foot long. But dead baitfish, especially oily, smelly ones like smelt or ciscoes, are used a great deal by pike fishermen. They appeal to the pikes' keen sense of smell more than do live baitfish.

You can fish your bait on a bobber rig or just cast it out and let it lie on the bottom. You can also cast it unweighted and give it a jerky retrieve to imitate a dying baitfish. Or, you can slow-troll it along the edge of a weedbed, using enough weight to keep it near the bottom.

Baitfish can be rigged with just a single hook, usually size 1/0 to 6/0, pushed through the nose. Be sure to attach the hook to a wire leader. You can also use baitfish on a quick-strike rig with one double or treble hook near the pectoral fin and the other near the dorsal. This way, you're able to set the hook immediately when a fish bites. Not only do you increase your hooking percentage, the fish don't have a chance to swallow the hook, so you can release them alive.

HOW TO BOBBER FISH FOR PIKE & MUSKIES

FEED LINE when your float goes under. In most cases, a pike or muskie grabs the bait sideways and starts swimming away. If it feels resistance, it may drop the bait. Pike and muskie often swim for a distance, then stop to turn the bait and swallow it headfirst.

SET THE HOOK when the fish starts moving again. Be sure that you've reeled up enough slack so you can feel the weight of the fish before setting. The time you must wait from the moment a pike or muskie takes your bait to the hook set varies from 30 seconds to 30 minutes, depending on the size of the baitfish.

Stream Trout

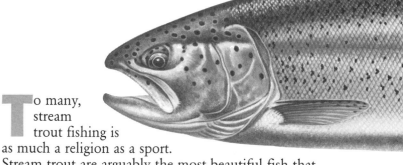

To many, stream trout fishing is as much a religion as a sport. Stream trout are arguably the most beautiful fish that swim in fresh water, and they're caught in some of the most beautiful settings.

There is a great deal of confusion surrounding the term "stream trout," because stream trout are also found in lakes. But those that inhabit lakes are not called "lake trout," they're still stream trout. Lake trout (p. 170) are a separate species found primarily in lakes.

Stream trout are coldwater fish. Whether they live in streams or lakes, they require cold, well-oxygenated water throughout the year. Stream trout dig their nests or *redds* in clean gravel in a stream; moving water is required to keep the eggs aerated. This explains why stream trout seldom reproduce in lakes and must be stocked.

Fishermen pursue four major stream trout species in North America. Brook trout are considered the easiest to catch. They favor water of about 54°F, and are rarely found where the water temperature exceeds 65°F. As a result, they usually live in the upper reaches of streams or near the

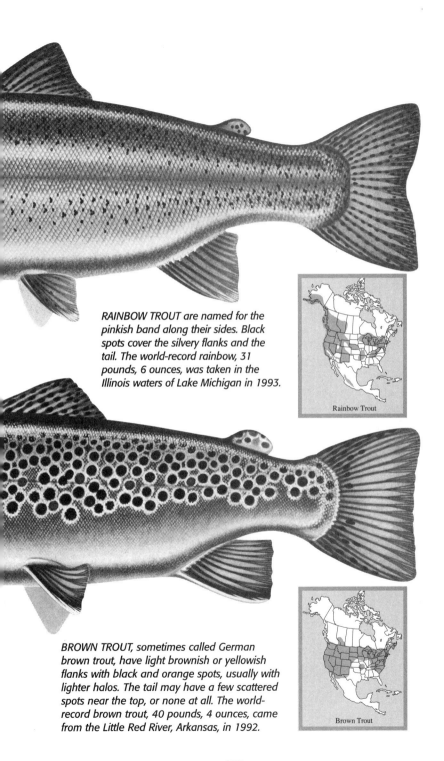

RAINBOW TROUT are named for the pinkish band along their sides. Black spots cover the silvery flanks and the tail. The world-record rainbow, 31 pounds, 6 ounces, was taken in the Illinois waters of Lake Michigan in 1993.

Rainbow Trout

BROWN TROUT, sometimes called German brown trout, have light brownish or yellowish flanks with black and orange spots, usually with lighter halos. The tail may have a few scattered spots near the top, or none at all. The world-record brown trout, 40 pounds, 4 ounces, came from the Little Red River, Arkansas, in 1992.

Brown Trout

mouths of tributaries. Rainbows prefer water of about 55°F, but are found in waters up to 70°F. They prefer relatively swift water. Cutthroats are found mainly in the West; they prefer the same water temperatures as rainbows. Brown trout, considered the most difficult to catch, favor water of about 65°F, but can tolerate temperatures as warm as 75°F. They sometimes live in warmer, slower-moving streams unsuitable to other trout.

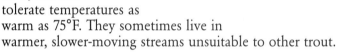

Stream trout rely heavily on insects for food, but small fish make up a large part of the diet of lake-dwelling stream trout. Small fish are also the major food for trout in warmer, marginal-quality streams. These waters have fewer trout, but are more likely to produce a trophy.

Trout are known for their wariness, and it's easy to understand why. In addition to man, many kinds of birds, mammals, crustaceans and other fish prey upon them. When alarmed, they immediately take cover beneath overhanging vegetation, undercut banks or fallen trees. Or they hide behind a boulder or in a deep pool.

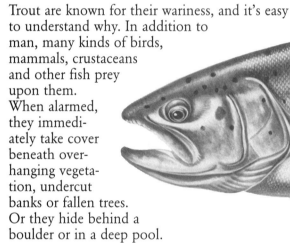

Large trout hooked in small streams are difficult to land. Fast, powerful swimmers, big trout instinctively dash for cover when hooked, often wrapping your line around a snag and breaking free.

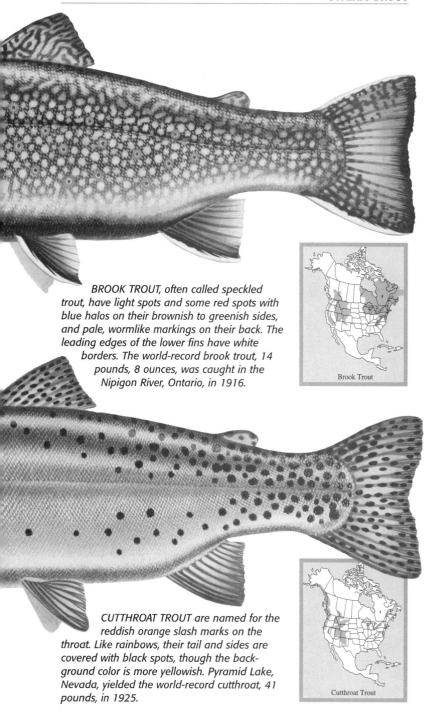

BROOK TROUT, often called speckled trout, have light spots and some red spots with blue halos on their brownish to greenish sides, and pale, wormlike markings on their back. The leading edges of the lower fins have white borders. The world-record brook trout, 14 pounds, 8 ounces, was caught in the Nipigon River, Ontario, in 1916.

Brook Trout

CUTTHROAT TROUT are named for the reddish orange slash marks on the throat. Like rainbows, their tail and sides are covered with black spots, though the background color is more yellowish. Pyramid Lake, Nevada, yielded the world-record cutthroat, 41 pounds, in 1925.

Cutthroat Trout

157

Where to Catch Stream Trout in Rivers & Streams

Most anglers would be amazed by the number of trout living in a typical coldwater stream. But the fish are seldom seen because they spend most of the day in cover. They show themselves only when they leave cover to find food.

As a rule, trout feed most heavily when the light is dim. Insect activity usually peaks during evening hours, leaving the stream teeming with prime trout food. So it's not surprising that many anglers prefer to fish late in the day.

During an insect hatch, trout may go on a feeding binge and catching them is easy. But not all insects hatch at the same time. The best strategy is to monitor the hatches on your stream and plan your fishing accordingly.

Water temperature also affects feeding activity. In spring, trout are most active in the afternoon when the water is warmest. Later in summer, they feed in the early morning when the water is coolest.

The largest trout are usually caught during peak feeding times. They keep smaller ones away from the best feeding spots. Small trout are forced to feed in areas that aren't quite as good.

Rising water may be a good indication that trout are feeding. Rains wash insects and other foods off streambanks and overhanging trees. As the stream rises and the current grows stronger, insect larvae and other morsels are dislodged from the bottom. Trout begin feeding when the swirling water carries food past their lies.

The best feeding lies are places where the natural flow of water gathers food. Examples are eddies, deep holes below rapids or waterfalls and shallow riffles. On warm, sunny days, trout may hold under shaded streambanks, eating food that falls or washes into the water.

When not feeding, trout seek shade and cover in resting areas beneath undercut banks and logs, below large rocks

CURRENT PATTERN determines distribution of trout in a stream. Trout will not waste energy constantly fighting the current, so they take cover in protected areas such as (1) eddies below boulders, (2) eddies that form beneath undercut banks on outside bends and (3) eddies that form below gravel bars.

or in deep pools. Even when resting, however, a trout will dart from cover to grab food as it drifts by.

Trout location may change during the year, depending upon water temperature. A stream with springs scattered along its course stays cold enough for trout all summer. But if spring-flow is confined to one section, the remainder of the stream may become too warm, concentrating the trout in water cooled by the springs.

Following is a list of some of the most important spots to find stream trout in moving water.

PRIME LOCATIONS IN STREAMS

•*Riffles* are excellent morning and evening feeding areas for trout. Riffles hold an abundance of insect life, but trout are hesitant to feed in riffles during the day, because they would be exposed to predators in the shallow water.

•*Runs* are deep, narrow, moderately fast-moving areas between riffles and pools. Runs hold good-sized trout most anytime, as long as they have adequate cover.

•*Pocket water* is shallow with many scattered boulders. The water may seem too shallow for trout, but the deep pockets that form below the boulders make excellent trout cover.

POCKET-WATER AREAS may seem too shallow for trout, but the deep pockets that form above and below the boulders often hold trout.

•*Deep pools* make good midday resting areas for medium- to large-sized trout. Pools are easy to recognize because their surface is smoother and the water looks darker than other areas of the stream.

•*Undercuts* usually form along outside bends from the force of the current cutting into the bank. They provide shade and overhead protection from predators and are most likely to hold trout in midday.

•*Plunge pools* at the base of a falls often hold the stream's largest trout. The force of the cascading water scours out a deep hole and creates an eddy that enables trout to escape the fast current.

Where to Catch Stream Trout in Lakes

Stream trout thrive in a variety of coldwater lakes, from tiny ponds to immense bodies of water such as Lakes Superior and Michigan. Because the fish require such cold water, however, most lakes do not have suitable habitat.

Most huge, deep bodies of water can support trout because their volume is so immense that the water never gets too warm. Lakes located at high altitudes or in the Far North also stay cool enough for trout all year. Most other small lakes and ponds, however, will not support trout unless they are spring-fed, because their water gets too warm in summer.

Two-story lakes (p. 19) have warmwater fish in their warm upper layer and trout in the depths. These lake are low enough in fertility that the depths contain adequate oxygen throughout the year.

In some lakes, trout populations are continually replenished by reproduction in tributary streams. However, stream trout cannot reproduce in most lakes and reservoirs, so they must be stocked.

Much of the year, trout remain near shore, feeding on minnows, insects and crustaceans. They sometimes school around food-rich inlets or near rock bars, sunken islands and points extending from shore. Their location, however, depends more on water temperature than on structure or bottom type.

During summer, trout may be forced deeper as the lake warms. They often squeeze into the narrow band of the thermocline because water below this point has too little oxygen. Although the surface water is warm, trout rise to feed on insects in early morning and late evening.

Compared to most gamefish, lake-dwelling trout are easy to catch. As a result, their numbers can be quickly reduced if fishing pressure is heavy. The best angling is in lightly fished waters where trout can grow for several years before they are caught.

Following is a list of some of the best locations to catch stream trout in lakes.

PRIME LAKE LOCATIONS

•*Gradually sloping shorelines* hold the most trout in deep, very cold lakes. The sun has a chance to warm the water along the shore, concentrating food and attracting trout.

•*Rocky points,* especially long, gradually sloping ones, are prime feeding areas in many trout lakes. Trout move up on the points in morning and evening to feed on hatching insects and forage for bottom organisms.

•*Stream mouths* are consistent trout producers in most types of trout lakes, because the inflowing water carries a variety of insect life.

•*The thermocline* may be the only suitable summertime habitat in some two-story lakes. The surface waters are too warm and the depths lack oxygen, so trout are forced into a narrow layer, usually at a depth range of 20 to 30 feet.

•*Weedbeds* provide the shallow-water cover that trout require. Trout are hesitant to leave weedy cover, because they become easy targets for predatory birds. The weeds also harbor insects, crustaceans and other foods.

•*Shallow bays* hold trout in early spring. Water in the bays warms much faster than that in the main lake, drawing minnows and starting insect hatches. When the bays warm, trout move back to the main lake.

How to Catch Stream Trout

Stream trout survive by being wary. Any sudden movement, shadow, noise or vibration will send them darting for cover. And once spooked, no amount of coaxing will get a trout to bite. If it is obvious that a trout has been disturbed, move on to another spot, because it may be a while before the fish resumes feeding. Because trout are so skittish, you must take extra care when approaching a trout's lie and presenting your lure.

When approaching the stream, for example, keep movement to a minimum. Study the water carefully to locate possible trout lies. Plan your fishing strategy before making the first cast. Wear drab colors, keep low and avoid open backgrounds. Because light rays bend at the water surface, trout can see all but the lowest objects along the streambank.

When wading, try to avoid scuffing the bottom, making large ripples or casting a shadow over the suspected lie of a trout.

FLY FISHING

Contrary to popular belief, fly fishing is not a mysterious art. The basic skills can be learned in a few hours. However, precision casting and a thorough knowledge of stream insect life take years of practice and study.

Artificial flies often resemble specific items in a trout's diet, from tiny insect larvae to large minnows. Most flies fall into one of four basic categories:

DRY FLIES. Resembling adult insects, dry flies float lightly on the water surface. They have a fringe of delicate feathers or hackle near the head that keeps them afloat. They are tied with or without wings. Dry flies are treated with a floatant to keep them buoyant.

WET FLIES. Tied with wings about the same length as the hook shank, wet flies resemble a variety of trout foods, including immature aquatic insects, drowned land insects, crustaceans or minnows. They are retrieved below

Tips for Fishing Dry Flies

TREAT your fly with a paste dressing so it floats high. Be sure the fly is dry before applying the dressing. If not, dry it with a desiccant powder.

CAST up and across the stream. Allow the fly to float downsteam naturally with the current. As the fly drifts, strip in any slack line.

AVOID DRAG. If the fly floats faster or slower than the current, it leaves a wake that gives it an unnatural appearance.

the surface. Hackles on wet flies are less prominent than on dry flies.

STREAMERS. Designed to imitate minnows, streamers are fished below the surface. The wings, made of feathers or hair, are longer than the body. Most streamers are brightly colored. Those made of hair are called *bucktails*.

NYMPHS. Nymphs are similar to wet flies and are intended to be fished beneath the surface. But unlike wet flies, they are tied without wings. They more closely resemble many of the immature insects found in streams. Because they are tied on relatively heavy hooks, they sink quickly. Some nymphs are weighted for an even faster sink rate.

QUICK TIP: Cast across current when using a wet fly or streamer. For deeper water, angle the cast slightly upstream so the fly can sink longer before the current sweeps it downstream. If you can't get deep enough, try a sinking line.

QUICK TIP: Twitch a streamer to mimic a darting baitfish by stripping in line. Wet flies are allowed to drift with the current or retrieved with a gentler twitching action.

TIPS FOR FISHING A NYMPH

CHECK FOR COMMON NYMPHS by stirring up the bottom, then holding a fine-mesh net downstream. Select a fly that resembles the most common insect.

ATTACH A STRIKE INDICATOR to your leader to help detect subtle takes. A strike indicator serves the same function as a bobber.

CAST DIAGONALLY upstream. Allow the nymph to drift naturally along the bottom. Watch the indicator and set the hook at any twitch or hesitation.

FISHING ARTIFICIAL LURES

Spoons, plugs, spinners and other artificial lures resemble minnows and attract the larger, fish-eating trout. Casting or trolling with such "hardware" enables you to cover a lot of water. If trout are feeding, they will usually hit the lure immediately.

> QUICK TIP: Angle your cast across current and upstream. Complete the retrieve before the line begins to bow downstream. The faster the current, the farther upstream you should angle the cast.

Thick, heavy spoons work best for casting, because you can toss them a long distance. But thin spoons are more effective for trolling, because they have a wider, more enticing wobble.

Small floating minnow plugs have a lifelike action that mimics a swimming shiner. Cast them upstream and work them downstream through riffles and runs, cast them along shallow lakeshores or troll them in open water.

> QUICK TIP: Practice the backhand flip to get your lure under low branches and other obstructions that are commonly present in stream-fishing situations. Use a sharp wrist snap to keep the lure low and on a straight trajectory.

Medium- to deep-diving minnow plugs and crankbaits work well for fishing deep pools in streams or fishing deep in lakes. Some of these lures dive to a depth of 20 feet or more. Jigs are also productive trout lures for fishing deep water.

Spinners used for trout fishing should have a freely turning blade. This way, the blade will spin even at a very slow retrieve speed.

Lake fishermen often attach cowbells, dodgers or other attractors in front of their lures for extra flash, which helps get the attention of trout scattered in open water. They also use planer boards to spread their lines horizontally and downriggers to place them at precisely the right depth.

There is no need for a delicate touch when fishing with artificials. Trout attack these lures aggressively, usually hooking themselves. Most fishermen use light- to medium-power spinning gear and 4- to 8-pound monofilament, but you may need 12-pound mono to handle large fish or to work snag-infested water.

FISHING WITH BAIT

Fishing with bait probably accounts for more trout than any other method. In spring and early summer when streams are high and clouded by runoff, it may be the only effective technique. Because trout have an excellent sense of smell, they can detect bait even when they can't see it.

A long rod, 7 to 9 feet, makes it easier to swing or drop the bait into hard-to-reach places. Choice of line depends on water clarity. Four-pound monofilament is best in clear water where trout spook easily. You can get by with 8-pound-test in muddy water. Most fishermen use size 6 to 8 light-wire hooks.

You may be able to gather bait such as worms, grasshoppers and nymphs as you walk along a stream or lakeshore. These baits are ideal, because they are more than likely part of the trouts' natural diet.

Bait selection is more critical for wild trout than for hatchery-reared trout, which are accustomed to eating dry pellets. Hatchery trout will take a variety of "grocery baits" including marshmallows, balls of cheese, corn and even baked beans.

In rivers and streams, bait is usually drift-fished. Still-fishing is more common in lakes. Anglers just toss out the bait on a slip-sinker rig and wait for a bite. Or, they fish it beneath a slip-bobber set at the same depth as the trout.

QUICK TIP: Hook the bait so it moves naturally in the current. Hook worms through the collar, minnows in the head and nymphs and grasshoppers just behind the head. Be sure the bait is fresh and lively. Add enough split shot about a foot ahead of the bait so the bait will tumble along the bottom, but not so much that it will hang up and stop drifting.

Steelhead

The fighting ability of steelhead is legend. They have been clocked at more than 26 feet per second, fastest of any freshwater fish. A hooked steelhead may leap repeatedly, sometimes clearing the surface by 2 to 3 feet. When you consider that they're often performing these acrobatics in swift water, it's not surprising that even the best steelhead fishermen land only a small percentage of the fish they hook.

Steelhead are rainbow trout that spend their adult lives at sea or in the open water of huge inland lakes, such the Great Lakes. Each spring, they migrate up tributary streams to spawn. Great Lakes steelhead may make a "mock spawning run" in fall, but no spawning takes place at that time. Along the Pacific Coast, steelhead may move into a stream in summer or fall and remain until spawning time the following spring. Steelhead can be found somewhere along the Pacific Coast every month of the year.

Pacific Coast steelhead were introduced into the Great Lakes in the late 1800s. Runs have since developed in many streams, especially those with clean, cold water and gravel bottoms. Because nonmigratory rainbows have also been stocked in the Great Lakes, fishermen sometimes mistake these deeper-bodied fish for steelhead.

Steelhead swim miles up tributary streams to find the right spawning area. They easily navigate raging cascades and most waterfalls. Only a dam or high waterfall blocks their progress.

While in the stream, steelhead bite reluctantly. The best technique is to drift-fish with yarn flies or spawn bags. By drifting a bait past a fish repeatedly, you can sometimes entice a take.

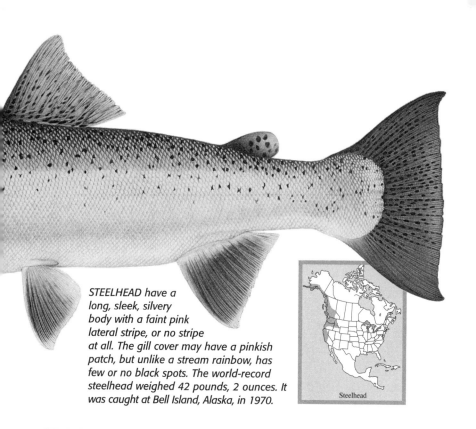

STEELHEAD have a long, sleek, silvery body with a faint pink lateral stripe, or no stripe at all. The gill cover may have a pinkish patch, but unlike a stream rainbow, has few or no black spots. The world-record steelhead weighed 42 pounds, 2 ounces. It was caught at Bell Island, Alaska, in 1970.

Steelhead

How to Drift-fish for Steelhead

MAKE a drift-fishing rig by attaching a 20- to 30-inch, 12-pound-mono leader to one eye of a 3-way swivel and a short, 8- to 10-pound-mono dropper to another. Pinch split shot onto the dropper and tie your main line to the remaining eye. Should you snag up, the shot will pull off the dropper.

USE a very long rod, from 8½ to 9½ feet, so you can handle up to 25 feet of line without casting. Using an overhand motion, just flip the line upstream and across current to reach the head of a likely looking run.

HOLD the rod tip high as the current tumbles your bait through the run. Cover the run thoroughly before moving. Set the hook whenever the bait stops drifting. Should you get snagged, pull on the line; the split shot will slide off the dropper, freeing the rig.

FOLLOW a hooked steelhead if it starts to run downstream. Wade carefully, watching for rocks or logs that could trip you. Exert as much pressure as your gear allows to keep the fish out of fast current.

Lake Trout

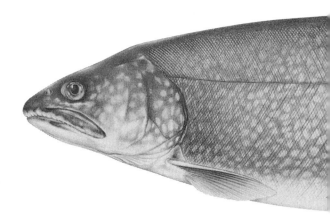

The prospect of battling a huge lake trout draws anglers to remote lakes as far north as the Arctic Circle. These waters, most of which are in Canada's Northwest Territories, yield many 30- to 40-pound lake trout each year and a few that are considerably larger. The biggest lake trout on record is a 102-pound giant netted in Saskatchewan's Lake Athabasca.

Lake trout prefer water from 48° to 52°F, colder than any other gamefish. They cannot survive in water warmer than 65°F. During summer, lake trout may descend to depths of 100 feet or more to find cold water. Many lakes have water cold enough for lake trout, but if the water is too fertile, the fish cannot make use of the deep, cold water, because it does not have sufficient oxygen. As a result, lake trout are restricted mainly to the cold, sterile lakes of the Canadian Shield, the Great Lakes and deep mountain lakes of the West.

Lake trout grow slowly in these frigid waters. In some lakes of northern Canada, a 10-pound laker might be 20

LAKE TROUT have light spots on a background varying from light green or gray to dark green, brown or black. The tail is deeply forked. The world-record lake trout, 72 pounds, was caught in Great Bear Lake, Northwest Territories, in 1995.

Lake Trout

SPLAKE, a lake trout/brook trout hybrid, have light spots on the sides and light, wormlike markings on the back. The tail is not as deeply forked as that of a lake trout and the tips of the tail are more rounded. World record: 20 pounds, 11 ounces; Georgian Bay, Ontario, 1987.

years of age or even older. The age of a trophy lake trout may exceed 40 years. Because they grow so slowly, they can be easily overharvested. To preserve the quality of their lake-trout fishery, many fishing lodges in the Far North are now requiring that all trophy trout be returned to the water.

Lake trout have excellent vision. But because so little light reaches the depths, they rely heavily on their sense of smell and their lateral line to find food. In some waters, they feed exclusively on aquatic insects, worms and crustaceans. In other lakes, they eat only fish: mainly ciscoes, whitefish, sculpins and smelt. Lake trout feed almost exclusively during the day, although shallow-water fish feed in dim light.

In the western states and parts of Canada, lake trout are known as Mackinaw or gray trout, although the most popular nickname is laker. A lake trout/brook trout hybrid, called the *splake,* has been stocked in some northern lakes, including Lakes Superior and Huron. Splake mature earlier than lake trout and grow faster than either parent, so they are less affected by fishing pressure.

Where to Find Lake Trout

Following ice-out, lake trout move from deep water into the warmer shallows, where they remain for several weeks until the water becomes too warm. Then they go as deep as necessary to find cold water. In lakes of extreme northern Canada, the shallows are always cold enough for lake trout, so they remain in water of 20 feet or less through the summer.

Lake trout move back to shallow water just before the fall spawning period. They spawn over a bottom of baseball-to football-sized rocks, usually at a depth of 5 to 20 feet. Because spawning lake trout are so easy to catch, most states and provinces close the season in fall.

Following is a list of some of the best spots to find and catch lake trout throughout the season.

PRIME LOCATIONS FOR LAKE TROUT

•*Narrows* between two major basins of the lake attract springtime lakers searching for food.

•*Extensions* from islands and points are ideal lake trout feeding areas in spring and fall.

•*Deep slots* and deep humps hold summertime lakers when the shallows become too warm.

•*Shallow reefs* that top off at 10 feet or less attract spawning lake trout in fall.

•*Rocky points* often attract small lake trout to shallow water on top of the points, while larger fish remain in deeper water off the tips.

•*River mouths* bring in warm meltwater that attracts lake trout. They are also drawn to schools of baitfish that hang around the plume.

•*Islands* that slope gently into deep water are excellent springtime laker spots. You'll usually find the fish at depths of 10 to 40 feet.

How to Catch Lake Trout

Lake trout anglers use a wide variety of techniques, depending mainly on the depth of the fish. When lakers move into shallow water in spring and fall, for instance,

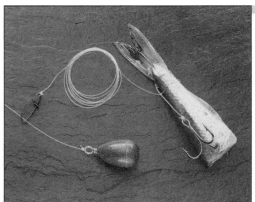

STILL-FISH WITH DEAD BAIT, such as a cisco or strip of sucker meat. Rig the bait on a size 1 to 2/0 hook and a slip-sinker rig with a ½- to 1-ounce egg sinker.

the best methods are casting with flashy spoons or still-fishing with dead bait. When they go deep in summer, vertical jigging or trolling with downriggers or 3-way swivel rigs are the most productive techniques. As a rule, lake trout use the same structure in winter as they do in summer. Jigging is, by far, the most productive method for catching lake trout through the ice.

> **QUICK TIP:**
> *Vertically jig with a vibrating blade, lead-head jig or heavy spoon. Use a graph to make sure you are right on top of the fish.*

Because lake trout water is usually free of snags, there is no need for heavy tackle. Most anglers use medium- to medium-heavy power spinning or baitcasting gear. Mono from 8- to 14-pound-test is adequate in shallow water. Spectra line, about 30-pound test, is a good choice for trolling or vertically jigging in deep water. It doesn't stretch and, because of its thin diameter, gets down easily.

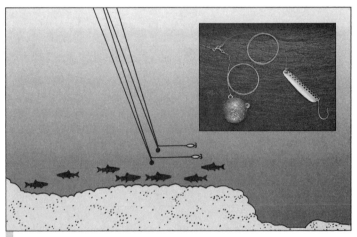

TROLL WITH DOWNRIGGERS to reach schools of deepwater trout. Note the depth of the trout on your graph and set your downrigger balls slightly shallower. Keep your "leads" no longer than 5 to 10 feet so the lures move up and down with the downrigger balls. If you don't have downriggers, you can troll with a 3-way sinker rig (inset) consisting of an 8- to 12-ounce sinker and a 2-foot dropper and a 6-foot leader. The dropper keeps your lure off bottom so it won't snag.

Salmon

Salmon are anadromous fish, meaning that they spend their adult life at sea and then return to freshwater streams to spawn. But scientists do not fully understand how a salmon can cross thousands of miles of open sea and then swim hundreds of miles up a freshwater stream to find the exact spawning site where its own life began. Many believe that they navigate at sea using the stars or the earth's magnetic field and then home in on their spawning stream using scent.

Five species of Pacific salmon – chinook, coho, pink, sockeye and chum – swim into streams from northern California to Alaska. Atlantic salmon enter streams from New York to Labrador.

Pacific salmon differ from Atlantics in that they have a fixed life span; most individuals of the same species return to spawn at the same age, and then die. Atlantics may live to spawn several times.

Pacific Salmon (combined)

Salmon are powerful swimmers; on the way to their spawning grounds, they commonly hurdle rapids and falls that would seem impossible to ascend. Because of their tremendous power, speed and stamina, salmon are considered by many anglers to be the ultimate sport fish.

For many years, fisheries agencies tried to stock Pacific salmon in

Atlantic Salmon

freshwater lakes, with little success. Then, in 1966, cohos were introduced into Lake Michigan in an attempt to control the lake's huge population of alewives and to create a new sport fishery. The salmon thrived on the small baitfish and the project's success led to the introduction of chinooks. Today, all of the Great Lakes support good salmon populations, and salmon have been stocked in many other large lakes. Chinooks are now plentiful in South Dakota's Lake Oahe and North Dakota's Lake Sakakawea, and many deep, cold lakes in the West have been planted with *kokanee,* the freshwater form of sockeye salmon. Landlocked salmon, the freshwater form of the Atlantic salmon, have been stocked in deep, cold freshwater lakes, mainly in the Northeast, since the late 1800s.

SOCKEYE SALMON have silvery sides with a brilliant steel-blue to bluish green back. They have no distinct black spots, but may have black speckles on the back. The normal life span is 4 years. World record: 15 pounds, 3 ounces; Kenai River, Alaska; 1987.

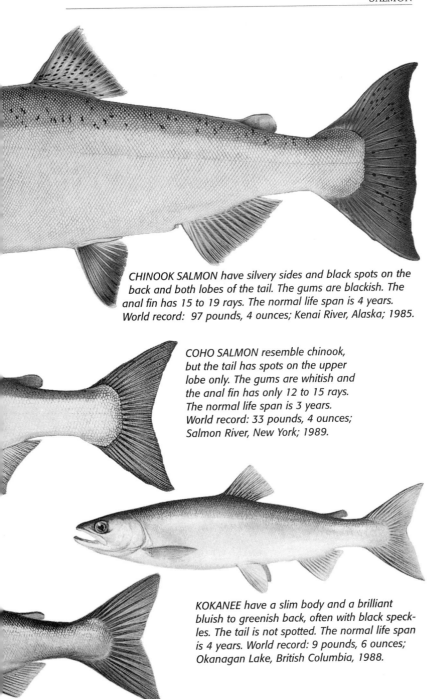

CHINOOK SALMON have silvery sides and black spots on the back and both lobes of the tail. The gums are blackish. The anal fin has 15 to 19 rays. The normal life span is 4 years. World record: 97 pounds, 4 ounces; Kenai River, Alaska; 1985.

COHO SALMON resemble chinook, but the tail has spots on the upper lobe only. The gums are whitish and the anal fin has only 12 to 15 rays. The normal life span is 3 years. World record: 33 pounds, 4 ounces; Salmon River, New York; 1989.

KOKANEE have a slim body and a brilliant bluish to greenish back, often with black speckles. The tail is not spotted. The normal life span is 4 years. World record: 9 pounds, 6 ounces; Okanagan Lake, British Columbia, 1988.

Salmon need cold water to survive, preferring temperatures around 55°F. In large lakes, wind and current move huge masses of water, causing drastic temperature changes over short periods of time. Salmon detect these fluctuations and follow water of their preferred temperature. As a result, salmon may be near the shore one day and miles away the next. Or, they can be schooling on the surface at sunrise and lying in 100-foot depths in the afternoon.

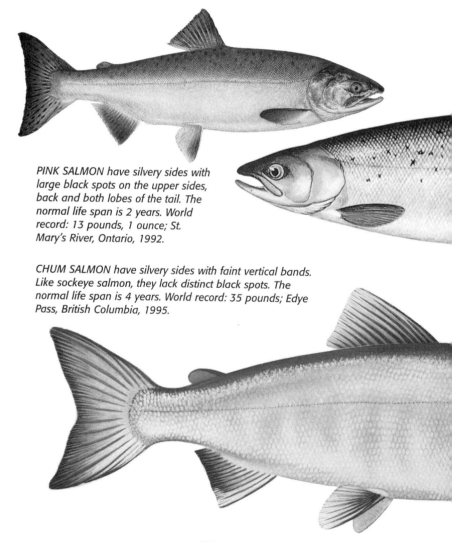

PINK SALMON have silvery sides with large black spots on the upper sides, back and both lobes of the tail. The normal life span is 2 years. World record: 13 pounds, 1 ounce; St. Mary's River, Ontario, 1992.

CHUM SALMON have silvery sides with faint vertical bands. Like sockeye salmon, they lack distinct black spots. The normal life span is 4 years. World record: 35 pounds; Edye Pass, British Columbia, 1995.

Coho and chinook salmon feed mainly on small fish, while kokanees and Atlantics rely more heavily on crustaceans and insects. The growth rate and ultimate size vary considerably among salmon species, with chinooks growing the fastest. In the Great Lakes, they commonly reach 20 to 35 pounds over a normal 4-year life span. Sea-run chinooks grow even faster, sometimes exceeding 50 pounds in 4 years.

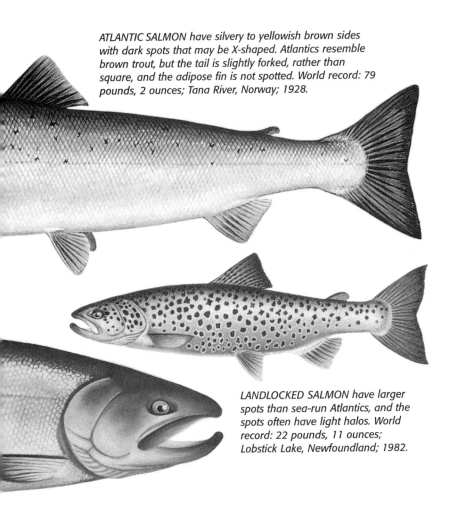

ATLANTIC SALMON have silvery to yellowish brown sides with dark spots that may be X-shaped. Atlantics resemble brown trout, but the tail is slightly forked, rather than square, and the adipose fin is not spotted. World record: 79 pounds, 2 ounces; Tana River, Norway; 1928.

LANDLOCKED SALMON have larger spots than sea-run Atlantics, and the spots often have light halos. World record: 22 pounds, 11 ounces; Lobstick Lake, Newfoundland; 1982.

Where to Catch Salmon

Salmon rely on cover and structure less than most other gamefish. They go where they must to find food and a comfortable water temperature.

In the Great Lakes, salmon schools are scattered during spring and early summer. Their search for 53° to 57°F temperatures may take them miles from shore or within casting distance of piers. Although fishing is excellent on some days, catching salmon consistently is difficult. But as spawning time nears, salmon gather near the mouths of spawning streams where finding and catching them becomes easier.

Stream mouths and power-plant discharges attract salmon, especially when surrounding water is too cold. The plume of warm water from the stream or discharge mixes with the cold water, creating a zone where the water temperature is ideal.

Stream fishing for salmon in Great Lakes tributaries begins in September and continues into October. Along the Pacific Coast, some fish enter rivers and streams as early as April, but the majority of the runs take place from June through September. Atlantic salmon return to fresh water from May through October, with some rivers having both spring and fall runs. Once salmon enter spawning rivers and streams, you'll find them in the same kinds of lies favored by trout (pp. 158-161).

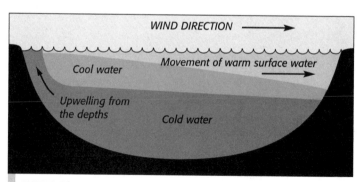

WINDS FORCE SALMON to move in order to stay at the right temperature. Onshore winds hold warm water along the shore; offshore winds push it out, and cold water wells up to replace it.

How to Catch Salmon

Salmon anglers use a wide variety of natural-bait and artificial-lure techniques. Natural baits are used extensively by West Coast salmon fishermen. Common bait-fishing techniques include still-fishing or drift-fishing with a gob of fresh spawn or a spawn bag and slow-trolling or *mooching* with herring. The latter technique involves dropping the bait to the bottom, then slowly raising and lowering it while the boat drifts.

In the Great Lakes, most anglers rely on artificials, particularly trolling spoons, plugs and flies, using side planers and downriggers to spread their lines and work a precise depth range. Silver or white lures with a little blue or green are good choices because they resemble alewives and smelt, important natural foods. But experienced anglers constantly experiment with different colors and actions, often trolling several different lures at the same time to determine the choice of the day.

For extra attraction, salmon fishermen often attach a large metal attractor, called a *dodger,* just ahead of their spoon or fly.

DOWNRIGGER FISHING

Trolling with downriggers and a good graph enables you to keep your lines in the fish zone most of the time. Downriggers also make it possible to fish deep water with relatively light tackle. If you had to add sinkers to get down, you would need a beefy rod to handle the weight.

Most salmon boats are equipped with at least two downriggers and many have four or more. This enables anglers to easily experiment with different depths and different lures until they find the right combination.

To reach the desired depth, simply attach your line (usually 12- to 20-pound mono) to a release device on the cable and then lower the downrigger ball into the fish zone. A strike frees the line from the release, so you can fight the fish without any extra weight. If desired, you can add another release farther up the cable and attach a second line, or *stacker*. You can also fish two lures on a single rod, each at a different depth, by using a "cheater" (below).

How to Rig a Cheater for Down-rigging

LOOP a rubber band to your line after letting it out, attaching it to a release and lowering the cannonball down about 10 feet. To prevent the rubber band from slipping, wrap it around the line twice, pushing one loop through the other, and cinch it tight.

RIG a cheater by running one end of an 8-foot monofilament leader with a second lure through the rubber band; clip the leader snap to your main line. The rubber band keeps the leader from sliding up and down the main line.

LOWER the cannonball to the desired depth. When a salmon strikes, the rubber band breaks. The cheater snap slides down the main line (arrow), pops the release and continues sliding until it jams against the lower lure. Now you have a direct pull on the fish.

Leader snap
Rubber band
Cheater (3 to 6 ft.)
Main line (3 to 6 ft.)
Release
Cannonball

FISHING WITH TROLLING BOARDS

Trolling boards keep your lines wide of the boat, a big advantage when fishing in clear, shallow water. Salmon are extremely boat-shy, so drawing the lines to the side of the boat's wake reduces the chance of spooking them.

QUICK TIP: Tie one end of a leader to the ring on a trolling spoon; the other end to a ball-bearing swivel. A snap swivel on the spoon would spoil the action.

The boards, which are pulled by cords attached to a pole in the boat, plane 40 to 75 feet to the side. The lines attach to release devices that slide down the cords toward the trolling boards. It is important to twist the line several times before attaching it to the release device; this way, the line won't slip through the release when a salmon strikes. Two or three lines can be fished off each side of the boat, covering a swath of water more than 100 feet wide.

Some salmon fishermen prefer side planers to trolling boards. Side planers, which are considerably smaller, attach directly to your fishing line, so there is no need for a cumbersome pole and cords. The drawback to side planers is that they stay on your line when you fight the salmon. This takes away from the sport and increases the chance of losing the fish.

QUICK TIP: Bend a spoon to improve its action by putting your thumbs together at its center, then sliding them outward while exerting pressure. The bend should be as smooth as possible. Spoons bent this way catch more water, causing them to veer more sharply to the side and creating a wider wobble.

SHORE FISHING

Salmon in the Great Lakes and other large inland waters spend only a small percentage of their time within casting range of shore. But if you carefully pick your times and places, you'll enjoy some fast salmon action.

Pre-spawn salmon begin congregating near stream mouths

weeks before the spawning run begins. They generally feed around the stream mouth for a few hours in early morning, move out in midday, and then return again in the evening.

Offshore winds also draw salmon into shore. It pays to carry a water thermometer and periodically check the temperature; as long as it's in the 53- to 57-degree range, there's a good chance the fish will be there.

Piers (below) give shore fishermen a big advantage, because they enable anglers to fish water they could not otherwise reach. Anglers also wade out on long points to reach salmon cruising far from shore.

Most shore fishermen use spinning rods at least 8 feet in length to power-cast heavy spoons. When the fish are tightly

HOW TO FISH FROM A PIER

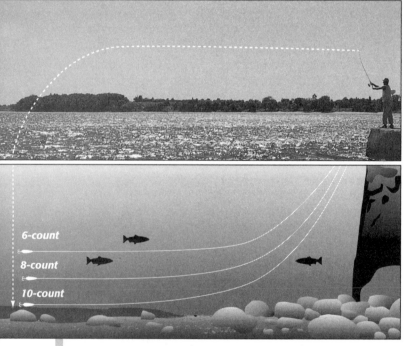

CAST A THICK SPOON as far as you can. Pay out line as the spoon sinks, counting until the lure hits the bottom. Then, reel in steadily. If the spoon hits bottom on a 10-count on the first cast, count down to 8 on the second cast, 6 on the third, etc. If you catch a salmon, count down to the same depth on the next cast.

schooled around stream mouths, still-fishing with a spawn bag or a live alewife on a slip-sinker rig may work better.

Use a large-capacity reel when shore-fishing for salmon. To ensure that a big salmon doesn't spool you, your reel should hold at least 300 yards of 12- to 17-pound-test mono.

RIVER AND STREAM FISHING

As Pacific salmon move into rivers and streams to spawn, their digestive tract begins to shrink and they stop eating. Their color changes from bright silver to reddish or brownish and finally to black. Males develop a strongly hooked lower jaw, or *kype,* and large canine teeth to help them defend their spawning territory. But even though the fish aren't feeding, they strike lures out of reflex or territoriality. Male Atlantic salmon also develop a kype but they continue to feed.

During the spawning run, certain pools and runs or the areas below dams and waterfalls literally become jammed with salmon. Once the fish reach their spawning grounds, it pays to concentrate on specific spawning beds, or *redds.*

When salmon are in slow to moderate current, most anglers cast with spoons, spinners and jigs. In faster current or when salmon are on the redds, try drift-fishing with yarn flies or spawn bags. In the large rivers of Alaska, salmon fishermen slip-troll with deep-diving plugs designed to get down to the bottom, where the majority of the fish are holding.

Although the majority of stream fishing is done by wading, drift boats offer some major advantages. The boat's swept-up ends make it easy to maneuver. As one person holds the boat steady with oars, another person casts from the bow. You can cover more water to find the fish, and, because you're drifting at the same speed as the current, drag on your lure is virtually eliminated. This makes it easier to get down to the fish.

QUICK TIP: Work the cover farthest downstream and closest to you first. Then, a hooked salmon will not spook others in unfished water when the current sweeps it downstream, or in unfished water close to you when you reel it in.

185

Releasing Fish

With fishing pressure on most bodies of water increasing, catch-and-release fishing is growing in popularity both as a fisheries management tool and as a voluntary measure among conservation-minded anglers. But the practice of catch-and-release is only effective if fish are properly handled before release.

As a rule, land fish as fast as possible. Allowing a fish to fight for an extended period will exhaust it and may cause a buildup of harmful lactic acids in its blood. The fish may swim away when released but it could die later from this buildup. To ensure that you don't needlessly tire a fish, choose a fishing line with a pound-test rating that allows you to put substantial pressure on the fish without breaking the line.

Another key to successfully releasing fish is keeping fish handling to a minimum. The best technique is to remove the hook from a fish's mouth without taking the fish out of the water. If you must hold a fish to unhook it, or if you want to take a quality photograph of your catch, wet your hands first to avoid removing the fish's protective slime layer.

Finally, try to limit the total amount of time a fish spends out of the water. If a hook is difficult to remove and you must hold the fish out of the water, periodically place it back in the water during the process. Don't attempt to rip out a hook that is deeply imbedded in a fish's throat or stomach. Instead, simply cut the line and allow a fish's strong digestive acids to dissolve the metal hook.

Fish are ready to be released when they can swim free from your hands as you cradle them gently under the belly. If they can't right themselves or if they don't have strong gill movement, be patient and give them more time to recover. Tips for reviving fish and other tips on releasing fish are shown on the next page.

Tips for Handling & Releasing Fish

REMOVE THE HOOK with pliers while the fish is still in the water. Using a hook with the barb pinched down makes these "water releases" very easy.

USE A FINE-MESH CRADLE (below) instead of a net when landing large northern pike and muskies. A cradle restricts the fish's movement, preventing it from injuring itself.

HOLD A BIG FISH horizontally with one hand in front of its tail and your other hand

beneath its belly (above). Holding a large fish vertically by the gills can cause the gill arch to tear.

RELEASE A FISH with its head facing into moderate current of a river or stream. Strong gill movement indicates that the fish is ready to be released.

GRASP BASS and other non-toothy fish vertically by the lower jaw. Never jaw-hold a fish at an angle because you could severely injure the fish's jaw.

REVIVE A FISH by gently rocking it back and forth. The fish is ready to be released when it can swim free from your hands and remain upright on its own.

187

Creative Publishing international, Inc.
offers a variety of how-to books.
For information write:
  Creative Publishing international, Inc.
  Subscriber Books
  5900 Green Oak Drive
  Minnetonka, MN 55343